The Collector's Encyclopedia of
Fiesta

Seventh Edition

Sharon and Bob Huxford

The Collector's Encyclopedia of
Fiesta

With Harlequin and Riviera

Seventh Edition

Sharon and Bob Huxford

COLLECTOR BOOKS
A Division of Schroeder Publishing Co., Inc.

The current values in this book should be used only as a guide. They are not intended to set prices, which vary from one section of the country to another. Auction prices as well as dealer prices vary greatly and are affected by condition as well as demand. Neither the Authors nor the Publisher assumes responsibility for any losses that might be incurred as a result of consulting this guide.

Searching For A Publisher?

We are always looking for knowledgeable people considered to be experts within their fields. If you feel that there is a real need for a book on your collectible subject and have a large comprehensive collection, contact us.

Additional copies of this book may be ordered from:

Collector Books
P.O. Box 3009
Paducah, KY 42002-3009

@$19.95. Add $2.00 for postage and handling.

Printed by IMAGE GRAPHICS, INC., Paducah, Kentucky

TABLE OF CONTENTS

ACKNOWLEDGMENTS

More than 25 years ago, something very exciting happened in our lives. We became collectors. It's an addiction, as any other collector will tell you. We were newlyweds, and if there was anything Bob thought I wanted, he either got it for me or helped me find it — within reason, of course. I went to a farm sale one day and came back with a beautiful pink glass butter dish. The butter dish, we soon found out, was the Sharon pattern in Depression glass, and when my mother unearthed a matching cake plate for me, I was hooked! I wanted more! So off we went, I guess this is where we established our pace. Our collection grew to several thousand pieces — ten patterns complete in service for six; all the cookie jars, salt and pepper shakers, water sets, candy dishes, butter dishes, and so forth we could get our hands on; children's sets; and some rare items like the Parrot pitcher and the red American Sweetheart tidbit tray.

Back then — this was the mid-sixties — being collectors didn't necessarily mean spending a lot of cash. But even then there were times we'd stretch the budget pretty thin just so we'd be able to buy glass. But what a wonderful time we had. It's virtually impossible for me to imagine what our married life would have been like had we not had this hobby together.

I don't think we're fickle, really, but came the early seventies, and we discovered Fiesta. It had color! Substance! We could actually use it! We were in love! Out went the Depression (in retrospect, a bad mistake — we should have packed it away), and in came the Fiesta and very soon a new interest — research. We found the lack of published material on our subject frustrating and dug in to learn all we could about it. We eventually made a connection with Collector Books and began an association with them that continues today. Since we wrote *The Story of Fiesta* back in 1974, we've also written on many other subjects — art, old books, decoys, advertising, and price guides every year — and because we do, we have to constantly stay on top of new areas of collecting interest as they develop. Our hobby has turned into a full-time business. But it suits us just fine — whether we're in the field gathering information or taking photographs or just on a 'for fun' vacation, either way we end up doing the antique shows, co-ops, and flea markets we like so much. No matter how much we enjoyed our Fiesta, we collected it in the early seventies; and just as the collectibles market itself changes as the years go by, so does the interest of anyone who follows it. Long ago, we sold most of our Fiesta (our second mistake), and our collecting diversified. So because we're no longer actively buying and selling, we find that we must rely on those that are in order to be able to offer a price guide that is valid and up to date. We want to take this opportunity to publicly thank those people who have contributed their time and knowledge for this survey. Without the splendid cooperation we receive from virtually anyone we ask, we would be without the kind of contact necessary to keep abreast of current developments and trends. Thank you all. In alphabetical order, these are the people who took part in this project, some by sending prices, others who contributed informational updates.

Aletha Barlow
Bill Beck
Betty Carson (Betty's Collectables)
Mick and Lorna Chase (Fiesta Plus)
Chuck and Margaret Denlinger (Dancing Girl)
Jack and Treva Hamlin
David Hanrahan
Grace Hines (Hines Sight)
Ralph and Jean Hinkle
Jack and Norma Kinion (White River Red's Antiques)
Steve and Annette Huffstetler

Leona B. Gonzales
Bob and Bonnie Koch (The Monument Shop)
Joe Langley
Gena Lightle (As Time Goes By)
William T. Mackall
Jack and Norma Majewski
Grace Means
Mary M. Mims
Carl Moore, Jr.
John Moses
Diane Petipas (Mood Indigo)

David Reardon
Michael Rosenburg
Terry Sfakis
Sam and Jennifer Skillern
Randy and Becky Stephens (Fiesta Texas)
E.S. Snow, Jr.
Terry Telford
Herbert Thompson
Aural Umhoefer
Ray Vlach
Ann Wise

An important contribution we want to remember was made by our late friend Austin Wilson and his wife Lucille. Many of the photos used for the sixth edition, our first hardback, were of items from their personal collection that they packed up and transported to our Evansville studio all the way from their home in Christiana, Pennsylvania. We enjoyed those few days with the Wilsons so much and were saddened to hear only a few months later that Austin had died. Those photos (taken by Donahue Studios) remain an important part of our seventh edition and serve in our minds as a memorial to a good friend and fellow collector.

Last but not least, we want to thank the Homer Laughlin China Company; our contact there over the years, Ed Carson; and you, our readers.

There were several others who responded to our contact letter and were willing to help us but for some reason or another further correspondence broke down. Whether on your part or ours, thanks anyway; we'll try you again next time.

Let us hear from you with your new finds, and if you have items we haven't yet shown, send photographs. We'll try to include them in the next edition. Until then, God bless you all with health, happiness, and wonderful friends. And whatever that special piece is you need to complete your collection, may you find not just one but a dozen.

THE LAUGHLIN POTTERY STORY

The Laughlin Pottery was formed in 1871 on the River Road in East Liverpool, Ohio — the result of a partnership between Homer Laughlin and his brother, Shakespeare Laughlin. The pottery was equipped with two periodic kilns and was among the first in the country to produce whitewares. Sixty employees produced approximately five hundred dozen pieces of dinnerware per day. The superior quality of their pottery won for them the highest award at the Centennial Exposition in Philadelphia in 1876.

In 1879 Shakespeare Laughlin left the pottery; for the next ten years Homer Laughlin carried on the business alone. William Edwin Wells joined him in 1889; and at the end of 1896, the firm incorporated. Shortly thereafter, Laughlin sold his interests to Wells and a Pittsburgh group headed by Marcus Aaron.

Under the new management, Mr. Aaron became President, with Mr. Wells acting in the capacity of Secretary-Treasurer and General Manager.

As their business grew and sales increased, the small River Road plant was abandoned, and the company moved its location to Laughlin Station, three miles east of East Liverpool. Two large new plants were constructed and a third purchased from another company. By 1903 all were ready for production. A fourth plant was built in 1906 at the Newell, West Virginia, site and began operations in 1907. In 1913 with business still increasing, Plant 5 was added.

The first revolutionary innovation in the pottery industry was the continuous tunnel kiln. In contrast to the old batch-type or periodic kilns which were inefficient from a standpoint of both fuel and time, the continuous tunnel kiln provided a giant step toward modern-day mass production. Plant 6, built in 1923, was equipped with this new type kiln and proved so successful that two more such plants were added — Plant 7 in 1927 and Plant 8 in 1929. The old kilns in Plants 4 and 5 were replaced in 1926 and 1934 respectively.

In 1929 the old East Liverpool factories were closed, leaving the entire operation at the Newell, West Virginia, site.

At the height of production, the company grew to a giant concern which employed 2,500 people, produced 30,000 dozen pieces of dinnerware per day, and utilized 1,500,000 square feet of production area. In contrast to the early wares painstakingly hand-fashioned in the traditional methods, the style of ware reflected the improved mass-production techniques which had of necessity been utilized in later years. The old-fashioned dipping tubs gave way to the use of high-speed conveyor belts and spray glazing, and mechanical jiggering machines replaced for the most part the older methods of man-powered molding machines.

In 1930 W.E. Wells retired from the business after more than forty years of brilliant leadership, having guided the development and expansion of the company from its humble beginning on the Ohio River to a position of unquestioned leadership in its field. He was succeeded by his son, Joseph Mahan Wells. Mr. Aaron became Chairman of the Board; his son, M.L. Aaron, succeeded him as President. Under their leadership, in addition to the successful wares already in production, many new developments made possible the production of a wide variety of utilitarian wares including the oven-to-table ware, Oven Serve and Kitchen Kraft. Later, the creation of the beautiful glazes that have become almost synonymous with Homer Laughlin resulted in the production of the colored dinnerware lines which have captured the attention of many collectors today — Fiesta, Harlequin, and Riviera.

On January 1, 1960, Joseph M. Wells became Chairman of the Board, and his son, Joseph M. Wells, Jr., followed him in the capacity of Executive Vice-President.

Homer Laughlin continues today to be one of the principal dinnerware producers in the world.

THE STORY OF FIESTA

In January of 1936, Homer Laughlin introduced a sensational new line of dinnerware at the Pottery and Glass Show in Pittsburgh. It was 'Fiesta,' and it instantly captured the imagination of the trade — a forecast of the success it was to achieve with housewives of America.

Fiesta was designed by Fredrick Rhead, an English Stoke-on-Trent potter whose work had for decades been regarded among the finest in the industry. His design was modeled by Arthur Kraft and Bill Bersford. The distinctive glazes were developed by Dr. A.V. Blenininger in association with H. W. Thiemecke.

This popularity was the result of much planning, market analysis, creative development, and a fundamentally sound and well-organized styling program. Rather than present to the everyday housewife a modernistic interpretation of a formal table service which might have been received with some reservation, HLC offered a more casual line with a well-planned series of accessories whose style was compatible with any decor and whose vivid colors could add bright spots of emphasis. Services of all types could be chosen and assembled at the whim of the housewife, and the simple style could be used compatibly with other wares already in her cabinets.

In an article by Fredrick Rhead, taken from the *Pottery and Glass Journal* for June, 1937, these steps toward Fiesta's development were noted: first, from oral descriptions and data concerning most generally used table articles, a chart of tentative sketches in various appealing colors was made. As the final ideas were formulated, they were modified and adjusted until development was completed. Secondly, the technical department made an intensive study of materials, composition, and firing temperatures. During this time, models and shapes were being studied. The result was to be a streamline shape, but not so obvious as to detract from the texture and color of the ware. It was to have no relief ornamentation and was to be pleasantly curving and convex, rather than concave and angular. Color was to be the chief decorative note; but to avoid being too severe, a concentric band of rings was to be added near the edges.

Since the early thirties, there had been a very definite trend in merchandising toward promoting 'color.' Automobiles, household appliances and furnishings, ladies' apparel — all took on vivid hues. The following is an excerpt from Rhead's article:

> The final selection of five colors was a more difficult job because we had developed hundreds of tone values and hues, and there were scores which were difficult to reject. Then there were textures ranging from dull mattes to highly reflecting surfaces. We tackled the texture problem first. (Incidentally, we had made fair-sized skeletons in each of the desirable glazes in order to be better able to arrive at the final selection.)

> We eliminated the dull mattes and the more highly reflecting glazes first, because in mass production practice, undue variation would result in unpleasant effects. The dull surfaces are not easy to clean, and the too highly reflecting surfaces show 'curtains' or variations in thickness of application. We decided upon a semi-reflecting surface of about the texture of a billiard ball. The surface was soft and pleasant to the touch, and in average light there were no disturbing reflections to detract from the color and shape.

> We had one lead with regard to color. There seemed to be a trade preference for a brilliant orange-red. With this color as a keynote and with the knowledge that we were to have five colors, the problem resolved to one where the remainder would 'tune in' or form appropriate contrasts.

> The obvious reaction to red, we thought, would be toward a fairly deep blue. We had blues ranging from pale turquoises to deep violet blues. The tests were made by arranging a table for four people; and, as the plate is an important item in the set, we placed four plates on various colored cloths and then arranged the different blues around the table. It seemed that the deeper blues reacted better than the lighter tones and blues which were slightly violet or purple. We also found that we had to do considerable switching before we could decide upon the right red. Some were too harsh and deep, others too yellow.

With the red and blue apparently settled, we decided that a green must be one of the five colors. We speedily discovered that the correct balance between the blue and the red was a green possessing a minimum of blue. We had to hit halfway between the red and the blue. We had some lovely subtle greens when they were not placed in juxtaposition with the other two colors, but they would not play in combination.

The next obvious color was yellow, and this had to be toned halfway between the red and the green. Only the most brilliant yellow we could make would talk in company with the other three.

The fifth color was the hardest nut to crack. Black was too heavy, although this may have been used if we could have had six or more colors. We had no browns, purples, or grays which would tune in. We eliminated all except two colors: a rich turquoise and a lovely color we called rose ebony. But there seemed to demand a quieting influence; so we tried an ivory vellum textured glaze which seemed to fit halfway between the yellow and the regular semi-vitreous wares and which cliqued when placed against any of the four colors selected. It took a little time to sell the ivory to our sales organization; but when they saw the table arrangements, they accepted the idea.

In the same publication a month earlier, Rhead had offered this evaluation of the popularity of the various colors with the public:

When this ware first appeared on the market, we attempted to estimate the preference for one color in comparison with the others. As you know, we make five colors . . . Because the red was the most expensive color, we thought this might affect the demand. And also, because green had previously been a most popular color, some guessed that this would outsell the others. However, to date, the first four colors are running neck and neck, with less that one percent difference between them. This is a remarkable result and amply bears out . . . that the 'layman' prefers to mix his colors.

Company price lists have always been our main source of information. Since our last edition, several more have been found; and these have clarified some misconceptions that resulted simply from not having them available for study. Our earliest is dated May 15, 1937; it lists fifty-four items. An article in the August 1936 issue of China, Glass, and Lamps reported new developments in the line since it had been introduced in January:

New items in the famous Fiesta line of solid-color dinnerware include egg cups; deep 8" plates; Tom and Jerry mugs; covered casseroles; covered mustards; covered marmalades; quart jugs; utility trays; flower vases in 8", 10", and 12" sizes; and bowl covers in 5", 6", 7", and 8" sizes.

By the process of elimination, then, in trying to determine the items original to the line, these must be subtracted from those on our May 1937 price list. A collector who has compiled the most complete assortment of company price lists that we are aware of tells us that the 10-oz. tumbler, the 6-cup (medium) teapot, and the 10½" compartment plate that are listed on our May '37 pamphlet were not yet listed on the Fall of 1936 issue which he has in his collection; so these would also have to be eliminated. These items remain, and until further information proves us wrong, we assume that they comprised the original assortment: coffeepot, regular; teapot, large; coffeepot, A.D.; carafe; ice pitcher; covered sugar bowl; creamer; bud vase; chop plate, 15"; chop plate, 13"; plate, 10"; plate, 9"; plate, 7"; plate, 6"; compartment plate, 12"; teacup and saucer; coffee cup and saucer, A.D.; footed salad bowl; nested bowls, 11½" to 5"; cream soup cup; covered onion soup; relish tray; compote, 12"; nappy, 9½"; nappy, 8½"; dessert, 6"; fruit, 5"; ash tray; sweets compote; bulb type candle holders; tripod candle holders; and salt and pepper shakers.

Adding to the selling possibilities of Fiesta, in June 1936 the company offered their 'Harmony' dinnerware sets. These combined their Nautilus line decorated with a colorful decal pattern, accented and augmented with the Fiesta color selected for that particular set. N-258 featured yellow Fiesta accenting Nautilus in white decorated with a harmonizing floral decal at the rim; N-259 used green Fiesta to complement a slender spray of pine cones. Red Fiesta, in N-260, was shown in company catalogs with Nautilus decorated with lines and leaves in an Art Deco motif (see Kitchen Kraft, Oven Serve for matching kitchenware items); and blue (N-261) went well with white Nautilus with an off-center flower-filled basket decal. These sets were composed of sixty-seven pieces in all. Of the Nautalis shape there were 9" plates (8), 6" plates (8), teacups and saucers (8), 5½" fruits (8), a 10" baker, and a 9" nappy. Fiesta items included 10" plates (8), 7" plates (8), 6" plates (8), a 15" chop plate, a 12" compote, one pair of bulb-type candlesticks, a pair of salt and pepper shakers, and a creamer and sugar bowl. Retail price for such a set was around $20.00. This offered a complete service for eight and extra pieces that allowed for buffet and party service for as many more in the contrasting items.

For some time during the earlier years of production, beautifully accessorized 'Fiesta Ensembles' were assembled — you will see a picture of a display ad showing such a set in the color plates. It contains 109 pieces, only 40 of which are Fiesta: 9" plates (8), 6" plates (8), teacups and saucers (8), and 5" fruits (8). Accessories included a 24-pc. glassware set with enameled Mexican motifs. There were eight of each of the following: 10-oz., 8-oz., and 6-oz. tumblers; color-coordinated swizzle sticks; and glass ash trays. A flatware service for eight with color-coordinated Catalin handles, a red Riviera serving bowl, a 15½" red Riviera platter, and a sugar and creamer in green Riviera completed the set. The flatware and glassware in these ensembles were manufactured by other companies and merely shipped to HLC to be distributed with the ensemble. Records fail to identify the company that may have manufactured these complementary accessories. Included in the packing carton was a promotional poster advertising this set for $14.95.

Originally all five colors sold at the same price; bud vases and salt and pepper shakers were priced in pairs. But on the May '37 price list, red items were higher than the other colors. For example, a red 12" flower vase was priced at $2.35; in the other colors it was only $1.85. A red onion soup was $1.00, 25¢ higher than the others. New to the assortment at that time were the three items mentioned earlier —- the 6-cup (medium) teapot, the 10½" compartment plate, and the 10-oz. tumbler. Bud vases and salt and pepper shakers were priced singularly.

A newly found mid-1937 price list tells us that the sixth color, turquoise, was added then and not in early '38 as we had previously reported. There is a 5" fruit on the May list; however, by mid-'37 the listing shows a 5½" and 4¾" fruit. Possibly the 5" and the 5½" are the same size fruit, with the so-called 5" listed actual size in mid-'37 due to the addition of the 4¾" size. (In comparing actual measurements to listed measurements, we have found variations of as much as ¾".) At this point, the first item had been discontinued; the 12" compartment plate was no longer available. The covered onion soup (evidently much more popular with today's collectors than it was then) was the second item to be dropped; by late that year it, too, was out of production. Two new items were added in the Fall of 1937, the sauce boat and the 11½" low fruit bowl. The assortment remained the same until the following July when the disk water jug and the 12" oval platter made their first appearance on company listings. No further changes were made until October 1939, when the stick-handled creamer was replaced by the creamer with the ring handle.

From 1939 through 1943, the company was involved in a promotional campaign designed to stimulate sales. This involved several special items, each of which was offered for sale at $1.00. An ad from the February 1940 *China, Glass, and Lamps* magazine provides us with the information concerning the campaign.

. . . dollar retailers in Fiesta ware include covered French casserole; 4-pc. refrigerator set; sugar, creamer, and tray set; salad bowl with fork and spoon; casserole with pie plate; chop plate with detachable metal holder; and jumbo coffee cups and saucers in blue, pink, and yellow.

But it also presents us with a puzzling question: what were the jumbo coffee cups and saucers? Sit 'n Sips perhaps? (See Miscellaneous.) The colors mentioned, though dark blue and yellow were in production in 1940, sound pastel with the inclusion of pink. Anyone have an answer? We don't!

Another item featured in the selling campaign is described in this message from HLC to their distributors:

> JUICE SET IN FIESTA . . . To help increase your sales! Homer Laughlin is offering an unusual value in the famous Fiesta ware . . . a colorful, 7-piece Juice Set, calculated to fill a real need in the summer refreshment field. The set consists of a 30-oz. disk jug in lovely Fiesta yellow, and six 5 oz. tumblers, one each in Fiesta blue, turquoise, red, green, yellow, and ivory. Sets come packed one to a carton, and at the one dollar minimum retail price are sure to create an upward surge in your sales curve. Dealers who take advantage of this Juice Set in Fiesta will find it a potent weapon in increasing sales of other Fiesta items. At a nominal price, customers who have not yet become acquainted with Fiesta can own some of the ware which has made pottery history during the past few years. The result? They'll want to own more!

Although the other promotional items are relatively scarce, the yellow juice pitcher is very easily found. This flyer is the only mention of it being for sale during this period; neither it nor the juice tumblers were ever included on Fiesta price lists. A few pitchers have been found in red, one in light green, and one in turquoise — perhaps dipped in error, on the whim of an employee, or for some special order we have no record of. In 1952 the promotion was repeated — the juice pitcher in gray, the tumblers in dark green, chartreuse, and Harlequin yellow. Either this issue was not extensively promoted or proved to be a poor seller judging from the scarcity of those items in these colors. Juice tumblers in rose are not at all rare, yet in this color they were not mentioned in either promotion. A factory spokesman explained this to us: while rose was not a standard Fiesta color until the fifties, it had been developed and was in use with the Harlequin line during the forties. Since it was available in the dipping department, it was used to add extra color contrast to the juice set.

The French casserole, individual sugar and creamer on the figure-8 tray, and the 9½" salad bowl were also never listed except in this promotion. Each is standard in a specific color; on rare occurrences when they are found in non-standard glazes, their values are at least doubled! French casseroles were all to be yellow; however, two dark blue bases and one complete casserole have been reported, and a lid and base have been found in green. (Before the fifth edition was published, we received a letter telling us that an ivory one existed. Having had no further correspondence with the owners, we wonder if this one could be the very rare footed version such as the one we report in the 'morgue' news.) Yellow was also standard for the 9½" salad bowl, but a very few have surfaced in dark blue, red, ivory, and light green. The individual sugars and creamers were to be yellow, the trays dark blue, but a few sugars and creamers have been found in turquoise; red creamers have been reported though they are very rare, and just recently a reliable, advanced collector assures us that his cobalt creamer is old Fiesta, not one from the new line. He explains that the cobalt is the lighter 'old' shade and that the piece is of the thinner gauge associated with the original. Trays in yellow or turquoise have been found, but these, too, are very rare.

One of the most exciting discoveries only recently unearthed and shown for the first time in this edition is the three-piece Fiesta Kitchenware Set referred to in the list of $1.00 promotions as 'casserole with pie plate.' See the Fiesta color plates for a look at this exciting set photographed with its original carton. We're sure it's authentic, since it was originally found in the unopened carton. The casserole is the one that has been a mystery for years. Though we suspected it to be a Homer Laughlin product years ago, the company rep didn't recall that they had ever produced such a casserole. However, before he retired, he sent us a Xerox copy of a promotional sheet verifying the casserole to be theirs. (See plate 9.)

Other items that have never been included on any known price list are the syrup pitcher, the very rare 10" flat cake plate, and the nested bowl lids that were mentioned in Rhead's article. A butter dish was never listed with Fiesta, but the consensus of opinion after so many years of collecting is that the Jade/Riviera butter dish (see plate 159 for more information) was dipped to go with the Fiesta line as well, since it may be found in cobalt and ivory, both standard colors in only one of HLC's lines, Fiesta.

More changes occurred in the Fall of 1942. Items discontinued at that time included the tripod candle holders, the A.D. coffeepot, and both the 10" and 12" flower vases.

In 1943 our government assumed control of uranium oxide, an important element used in the manufacture of the Fiesta red glaze. As a result, it was dropped from production — 'Fiesta red went to war.' Perhaps the fact that Fiesta red had been listed separately and priced proportionately higher than the other colors was due to the higher cost of raw material plus the fact that the red items required strict control during firing; losses that did occur had to be absorbed in the final costs.

The color assortment in 1944 included turquoise, green, blue, yellow, and ivory. The nested bowls no longer were listed. The rate of price increases over the seven years Fiesta had been on the market is hard for us to imagine: ash trays were still only 15¢, egg cups were up to 35¢ from 30¢, relish trays were up only 15¢ to $1.80 complete.

Although the colors are listed the same on the 1946 price list, the following pieces were discontinued: bud vase, bulb-type candle holders, carafe, 12" compote, sweets compote, 8" vase, 11½" fruit bowl, ice pitcher, marmalade and mustard, 9½" nappy, relish tray, footed salad bowl, large teapot, 10-oz. tumbler, and utility tray.

A recently reported price list from November 15, 1950, helps us pinpoint the time of the radical color change that had taken place by October of 1951. Though the 1950 price lists still offered the original colors, by fall of 1951 light green, dark blue, and old ivory had been retired; their replacements were forest green, rose, chartreuse, and gray. Turquoise and yellow continued to be produced. These new colors have been dubbed 'fifties colors,' since they and the listed assortment remained in production without change until 1959.

Prices listed in 1956, twenty years after Fiesta was introduced, were higher, of course; but still the increase is so slight as to be quite noteworthy to us in the nineties. Ash trays sold for 40¢, teacups that were 25¢ were up to 65¢. Dinner plates had little more than doubled at 90¢, and coffeepots sold for $2.65. They, too, had about doubled in price.

The big news in 1959 was, of course, the fact that Fiesta red was reinstated. It was welcomed back with much ado! The Atomic Energy Commission licensed the Homer Laughlin China Company to again buy the depleted uranium oxide, and Fiesta red returned to the market in March of 1959.

In addition to red, turquoise, and yellow, a new color — medium green — was offered. Rose, gray, chartreuse, and dark green were discontinued; and the following items were no longer available: 15" chop plate, A.D. coffee cup and saucer, regular coffeepot, 10½" compartment plate, cream soup cup, egg cup, 4¾" fruit bowl, and the 2 pt. jug. A new item made an appearance — the individual salad bowl.

By 1961 the 6" dessert bowl was no longer listed. Aside from that change, the line and the color assortment remained the same. Though retail prices had risen in 1965; by 1968 some items stayed the same while others actually dropped slightly.

In the latter months of 1969 in an effort to meet the needs of the modern housewife and to present a product that was better designed to be in keeping with modern day decor, Fiesta was restyled. Only one of the original colors, Fiesta red — always the favorite — continued in production (see chapter on Fiesta Ironstone).

The big news of 1986 was the exciting new line of Fiesta ware that was introduced in the Spring. How better to celebrate its fiftieth birthday! We'll tell you all about it in one of the following chapters.

THAT RADIOACTIVE RED

Exactly when the first rumors began circulating, hinting that the red Fiesta could be 'hazardous' to your health, is uncertain. In most probability, it was around the time that Fiesta red was reintroduced after the war and was no doubt due to the publicity given to uranium and radioactivity during the war years. Clearly another case where 'a little learning can be a dangerous thing.'

In any case, this worry must have remained to trouble the minds of some people for several years. Even today the subject comes up occasionally and remains a little controversial, though most folks in this troubled age of acid rains, high unemployment, cholesterol-free diets, and constant reminders that 'cigarettes are hazardous to your health' don't really seem too upset by it anymore.

The following letter appeared in the *Palm Beach Post Times* in February 1963. It was written tongue-in-cheek by a man who had evidently reached the limit of his patience. HLC sent it to us from their files; it has to be a classic.

> Editor:
> After reading about the radioactive dishes in your paper, I am greatly concerned that I may be in danger, as I had a plate with a design in burnt orange, or maybe it was lemon.
> This plate was left to me by my great-grandmother, and I noticed that whenever she ate anything from it, her ears would light up; so we all had to wear dark glasses when dining at her house.
> I first became suspicious of this dish when putting out food for my dog on it I noticed the dog's nose became as red as Rudolph's; and one day a sea gull fed from it, and all his feathers fell off; then one night when the weather was raw I placed it at the foot of my bed, and my toenails turned black.
> Using it as a pot cover while cooking eel stew, the pot cracked; and reading the letters in your paper last week have concluded I am not the only person having a cracked pot in the house; so perhaps some of your other readers used a plate for a cover.
> I finally threw this plate overboard at a turn in the channel, now a buoy is no longer needed there, as bubbles and steam mark this shoal.
> Will you please ask your Doctor or someone if they think this plate is radioactive, and if so am I in any danger, and if so from what?
>
> (Name Withheld)

Several years ago we were allowed the opportunity to search through old company literature in the event that some bit of pertinent information had escaped our notice. It was obvious from letters contained in these files that HLC had always been harassed with letters from people concerned with the uranium content of the Fiesta red glaze. Their replies were polite, accommodating, and enlightening. Here in part is one of their letters:

> Before 1943 the colorant (14% by weight of the glaze covering the ware) is uranium oxide (U-308), with the uranium content being made up of about 0.7% U-235 and the remainder U-238. Between 1943 and 1959 under license by AEC, we have again been producing a red glazed dinnerware. However the colorant now used is depleted technical grade U-308 with the uranium content being made up of about 0.2% U-235 and the remainder U-238.

Studies were conducted for us by Dr. Paul L. Ziemer and Dr. Geraldine Deputy (who is herself an avid Fiesta collector) in the Bionuclionics Department of Purdue University. The penetrating radiation from the uranium oxide used in the manufacturing of the glaze for the red Fiesta ware was measured with a standard laboratory Geiger Counter. All measurements are tabularized in units of milliroentgens per hour (mR/hr).

ITEM	SURFACE CONTACT	4" ABOVE SURFACE	ALONG RIM
13" Chop Plate	0.8	0.35	0.1
9" Plate	0.5	1.5	0.07
Fruit Bowl	1.5	0.5	0.1
Relish Tray Wedge	0.8	0.2	0.02
Cup	1.3	0.2	0.03

In order to compare the above values to familiar quantities of radiation, we calculated the exposure of a person holding a 13" chop plate strapped to his chest for twenty-four hours. This gives twenty milliroentgens per day. Safe levels for humans working with radiation is one hundred milliroentgens per week for a five-day week or twenty milliroentgens per day as background radiation.

Some other measurements of interest for comparison purposes are:

ITEM	RADIATION
Radium Dial on a Watch	20mR/hr
Chest X-Ray	44 mR per film
Dental X-Ray	910 mR per film
Fatal Dose	400,000 mR over whole body

So you see — unless you've noticed your grandmother's nose glowing — we're all quite safe!

One other small worry to put to rest (some have mentioned it): there is no danger from the fired-on glazes, which are safe as opposed to a shellac-type color which could mix with acid from certain foods and result in lead poisoning.

Back in May of 1977 on an Eastern television station, an announcement was made concerning the pros and cons of the safety of colored-glazed dinnerware. Fiesta was mentioned by name. We contacted the Department of Health, Education and Welfare, FDA, in Chicago, Illinois. This in part is their position, and it is supported by HLC:

The presence of lead, cadmium, and other toxic metal in glaze or decal is not in itself a hazard. It becomes a problem only when a glaze or decal that has not been properly formulated, applied, or fired, contains dangerous metals which can be released by high-acid foods such as fruit juices, some soft drinks, wines, cider, vinegar, and vinegar-containing foods, sauerkraut, and tomato products.

HLC passed the rigorous federal tests with flying colors! In fact, the only examples of earthenware posing a threat to consumers were imported, and hobbyists were warned to use extreme caution in glazing hand-thrown ceramics.

The FDA report continues:

Be on the safe side by not storing foods or beverages in such containers for prolonged periods of time, such as overnight. Daily use of the dinnerware for serving food does not pose a hazard. If the glaze or decal is properly formulated, properly applied, and properly fired, there is no hazard.

...R.I.P.

IDENTIFICATION OF TRADEMARK DESIGN AND COLOR

Fiesta's original design, colors, and name are the registered property of the Homer Laughlin China Company. Patent No. 390-298 was filed on March 20, 1937, having been used by them since November 11, 1935. With only a few exceptions, their distinctive trademark appears on every piece. These four seem to be the most common.

The indented trademark was the result of in-mold casting; the ink mark was put on with a hand stamp after the color was applied and before the final glaze was fired.

As many other manufacturers were following the trend to brightly colored dinnerware, the wide success and popularity of Fiesta resulted in its being closely copied and produced at one time by another company. Homer Laughlin quickly brought suit against their competitor and forced the imitation ware to be discontinued. To assure buyers they could buy with complete confidence, the word 'Genuine' was added to the hand stamp sometime before 1940. Genuine Fiesta was the exclusive product of Homer Laughlin.

There are some items in the Fiesta line which were never marked —- juice tumblers, demitasse cups, salt and pepper shakers, and some of the Kitchen Kraft line. The teacups were never to have been marked as a standard procedure, but a rare few of these and the demitasses as well have been found with the ink stamp. Sweets compotes, ash trays, and onion soups may or may not be marked. Never pass up a 'goodie' such as these simply because they are unmarked! As you become more aware of design and color, these pieces will be easily recognized as Fiesta.

Fiesta's design is very simple and therefore very versatile. The pattern consists of a band of concentric rings graduating in width, with those nearer the rim being more widely spaced. The rings are repeated in the center motif on such pieces as plates, nappies, platters, desserts, etc. Handles are applied with slight ornamentation at the base. Vases and tripod candle holders, though designed without the rings, are skillfully modeled with simple lines, geometric forms, and stepped devices that instantly relate to the Art Deco mood of Fiesta's clean uncluttered shapes. Flat pieces and bowls are round or oval; hollowware pieces are globular, and many are styled with a short pedestal base decorated with the band of rings.

But, of course, it's Fiesta's vivid colors that first capture your attention. The wide array of color provides endless possibilities for matching color schemes and decor. And if you find you love all eleven, you'll surely enjoy collecting a place setting in every color — Fiesta red, yellow, rose, old ivory, gray, dark blue, turquoise, forest green, light green, medium green, and chartreuse.

DATING CODES
AND ENGLISH
MEASUREMENTS

Many HLC lines often carry a backstamp containing a series of letters and numbers. The company has provided this information to help you in deciphering these codes:

In 1900 the trademark featured a single numeral indentifying the month, a second single numeral identifying the year, and a numeral 1, 2, or 3 designating the point of manufacture as East Liverpool, Ohio.

In the period 1910 –20, the first figure indicated the month of the year, the next two numbers indicated the year, and the third figure designated the plant. Number 4 was 'N,' Number 5 was 'N5,' and the East End plant was 'L.'

A change was made for the period of 1921–1930. The first letter was used to indicate the month of the year such as 'A' for January, 'B' for February, 'C' for March. The next single digit number was used to indicate the year, and the last figure designated the plant.

For the period 1931– 40, the month was expressed as a letter; but the year was indicated with two digits. Plant No. 4 was 'N,' No. 5 was 'R,' No. 6 and 7 were 'C' and No. 8 was listed as 'P.' During this period, E-44R5 would indicate May of 1944 and manufactured by Plant No. 5. The current trademark has been in use for approximately seventy years, and the numbers are the only indication of the specific years that items were produced.

Collectors have long been puzzled over the origin and meaning of such terms as oval 'baker' and '36s bowl' — not to mention the insistent listings of 4" plates, when it has become very apparent that 4" plates do not exist! We asked our contact at HLC for an explanation. He told us that each size bowl was assigned a number. Smaller numbers indicated larger bowls, and vice versa. The word 'baker' as used to describe a serving bowl was an English potting term. It was also the English who established the unfortunate system of measurements based on some rather obscure logic by which a 6" plate should be listed as 4". The 7" 'nappies' (also an English term) actually measure 8¾"; 4" fruits are usually 5½"; and 6", 7", and 8" plates are in reality 7", 9", and 10".

This practice continued through the fifties (though more in connection with other HLC lines than Fiesta) until it became so utterly confusing to everyone involved that actual measurements were thankfully adopted. However, these may vary as much as ¾" from those listed on company brochures. For instance, 9" and 10" plates actually measure 9½" and 10½", and the 13" and 15" chop plates are 12¼" and 14¼".

The small incised letters and/or numbers sometimes found on the bottom of hollowware pieces were used to identify a pieceworker — perhaps a molder or a trimmer — and were intended for quality control purposes. More likely to appear on Harlequin, these are sometimes seen on Fiesta as well.

FREDRICK HURTEN RHEAD

The Rhead family was prominent among the finest ceramists of nineteenth-century England. Fredrick Hurten Rhead came from a long line of English Stoke-on-Trent potters and must without doubt be considered one of the most productive artisans in the history of the industry. At the age of 19, he was named Art Director at the Wardel Pottery. After leaving his home in Staffordshire in 1902, he worked at the Vance/Avon Faience Co., in Tiltonville, Ohio, for a term of about six months before moving on to the Weller Pottery in Zanesville, Ohio. By 1904 he was awarded the position of Art Director at the nearby Roseville Pottery. The many lines of artware he produced for these companies earned him widespread recognition. Inspired by nature and influenced by both Art Nouveau and the Arts and Crafts Movement, he became well known for dramatic sgraffito work, which he executed in intricate detail. An element he often favored was a stylized tree, variations of which he used frequently throughout his career. In later years, he designed a set of nested mixing bowls for Homer Laughlin; they were decorated with embossed trees reminiscent of his earlier work.

Leaving Roseville in 1908, he went to the William Jervis Pottery on Long Island. In 1909 he accepted the post of Instructor in Pottery at the University City Pottery in Saint Louis. From 1911 to 1913 he was associated with the Arequipa Pottery in Fairfax, California. There, with the assistance of his wife, Agnes, he taught ceramics to patients at the Arequipa Sanatorium. Leaving Arequipa, he organized the Pottery of the Camarata in Santa Barbara, later to be incorporated as The Rhead Pottery. Never a confident thrower, Rhead involved himself fully with developing new glazes. One of his finest achievements was Mirror Black, a recreation of the sixteenth-century black-glazed pottery of the Orient, which earned him a Gold Medal at the 1915 San Diego Exposition.

In December of 1916, Rhead published *The Potter*, a monthly magazine dealing with the progress of the industry. The editor of the historical department was Edwin A. Barber, whose death was reported in the third issue (February, 1917). With that the paper was abandoned.

Freed of the pressures he had felt at the commercial potteries in Ohio, Rhead utilized this time to develop his creative capabilities to their fullest, but as a business man he was unable to keep his pottery afloat. He encountered financial difficulties, and his pottery failed. Returning to Zanesville in 1917, he joined the American Encaustic Tiling Company. Loiz Whitcomb, a fellow artisan from his California pottery (with whom he had fallen in love after his first marriage was annulled), came back to the midwest to join him; they soon married. Rhead served at AE Tile as Director of Research. In 1927 he moved to the Homer Laughlin Company where he designed his famous dinnerware line, Fiesta. He remained there until his death in 1942. No other ceramic artist made more of an impact on this country's pottery industry. From the early days of his career to the last, Rhead's work evolved effortlessly, leaving behind a legacy still enjoyed by thousands today.

Shown below are examples of only two of the lines Rhead developed for Roseville and Weller — Della Robbia on the right, Weller Rhead Faience on the left.

FIESTA

Plate 1

Comprised of a red footed salad bowl and twelve Tom and Jerry mugs in hard-to-find and now very costly medium green, this Christmas punch bowl set is brightly festive. This may have been a department store promotion or a combination chosen by an individual to fill holiday party needs — nothing exists to suggest it was marketed as such by HLC.

Plate 2

Ash Tray. These were made from 1936 until the Fiesta Ironstone line was discontinued in 1973, and they can be found in all of the old colors plus Turf Green and Antique Gold. These are 5½" in diameter.

Plate 3

Covered Onion Soup Bowl (left foreground). Imagine a lifestyle that required these. If the number that remains to the present day is any indication, the housewives of the thirties found them to be a little ostentatious, too. They can be found in red, ivory, dark blue, light green, yellow, and turquoise. They're very scarce, especially in turquoise. A newly-found company price list contains information that easily explains this. Turquoise was added to the color assortment in mid-'37, and by Fall of that year the onion soup had been discontinued. Only a few collectors report ever having seen one that was marked. (See chapter on Identification of Trademark, Design, and Color for list of items that were never or rarely ever marked.)

Dessert Bowl (upper left). This is another item that was in the original line. It was produced until 1961 in all colors; it's scarce in medium green. They're 6" in diameter.

Individual Salad Bowl (center back). A later addition, these were not produced until 1959 and were, of course, only made in the colors of that period — red, turquoise, yellow, and medium green. Occasionally you may find one with no rings in the bottom, probably produced toward the transition into Fiesta Ironstone when such modifications were finalized. They're easier to find in red and medium green; nevertheless, expect to pay a premium for medium green, regarded by collectors as Fiesta's 'rare color.'

Fruit Bowl, 5½" (upper right). Probably the bowl listed as 5" in the original assortment, this item was made until the restyling in 1969 and is available in all eleven colors.

Fruit Bowl, 4¾" (right foreground). This was probably the bowl that was added to the assortment in mid-'37. We have price lists that are dated 1956 and 1959; they show it as still available in 1956, but it does not appear on the 1959 price list when medium green was introduced, and only a few have been found in this color. It's rather scarce in red as well.

Plate 4

Cream Soup Bowl. These were part of the original line and continued to be made until sometime in 1959. They're found in all colors but are very rare in medium green, the newcomer to the color assortment that year.

Plate 5

Footed Salad Bowl (left). These not only hold salad for more people than you'd probably care to entertain but make great punch bowls, too. They're rather hard to come by. They were made from the time Fiesta was introduced until 1946 in only the first six colors with ivory and yellow reported to be the hardest to find. They're listed as being 12" but are actually 11¼" in diameter.

Plate 1

18

Plate 2

Plate 3

Plate 4

Plate 5

Fruit Bowl (right). These are hard to find, especially in red. They were made from 1937 until sometime between 1944 and 1946 in the six original colors. They're shallow, only 3" deep and 11¾" in diameter.

Plate 6
    This photo is for all of you who are nested bowl collectors. We wanted to show you just how fantastic the completed collection looks.

Plate 7
    Mixing Bowls. Stacked together, this set weighs almost twenty pounds. They were made in only the original six colors, since they were in production from 1936 until around 1943. Each bowl is numbered in sequence on the bottom, #1 being the smallest. They range in size from 5" to 11½". The only bowl lids ever officially offered on a company price list were the four smaller sizes. Although the list we refer to is undated, we can place it after August 1936 (our price list bearing that date makes no mention of them) and before 1937 (because turquoise was not yet being offered on the list in question).

Plate 8
    Bowl lids are extremely rare in any size, but the #5 shown here remained undiscovered until just before our 1994 update. Since then, a #6 has surfaced — but as far as we know, there's only one! (Photography © Adam Anik)

Plate 6

Plate 7

Plate 8

Plate 9

Promotional Casserole and Pie Plate. For many years collectors have suspected that these casseroles might have been made by Homer Laughlin, since they are found in several colors that match HLC's standard glazes. Most of them are red, turquoise, yellow, light green, and mauve blue, though cobalt, Harlequin yellow, and spruce green have also been found. Even though years ago the company denied they ever produced them, the evidence available today contradicts that statement. This set was recently found in the original unopened carton which is stamped Fiesta on the side not shown in the photo. And not long ago we received from the company a Xerox of original material showing this casserole in a metal frame. An artist's rendering is shown in the chapter entitled Go-Alongs. So, though no examples have ever been reported with the HLC mark, we feel sure that this is the 'casserole with pie plate' offered in the promotional campaign of 1939–1942 for the price of only $1.00 per set. The casserole is 3" deep and measures 8" in diameter. The Fiesta Kitchen Kraft pie plate is 9¾" (the smaller of the two shown later in the Kitchen Kraft section).

Plate 10

Nappy, 9½" (left). This item was part of the original assortment and is still listed on our 1944 price list, but by Fall of 1946 it was no longer available.

Nappy, 8½" (center). This bowl was made from 1936 until the line was restyled in '69, so it comes in all 11 colors.

Unlisted Salad Bowl (right). Although this salad bowl was never listed on the price pamphlets, a trade paper from 1940 reported on the Homer Laughlin sales campaign that offered this bowl accompanied by the Kitchen Kraft spoon and fork for only $1.00. The ad copy indicated that these bowls were yellow. They're scarce even in that color, and only a rare few have been reported in ivory, red and dark blue (See Plate 13). Collectors have fallen into the habit of referring to these as the 'unlisted salad bowl.' They're 3¾" deep by 9½" in diameter.

Plate 11

French Casserole (left). One of the eight special campaign items offered by HLC from 1939 to '42, the French casserole is a relatively scarce item. Virtually all are yellow. Two bases and one complete unit have been reported in dark blue, and a lid and base have been found in light green.

Casserole (right). Considering that production of the covered casserole was continuous from 1936, they're not especially easy to find. Examples in medium green and the fifties colors are most desirable. An oddity has been reported — a collector has sent us a photo of a casserole bottom in the copper-bronze luster like the demitasse pot in Plate 17.

Plate 12

Tricolator Bowl. This is the casserole bottom without the standard applied foot. It's another piece the company denied making, but collectors just don't buy it. It's marked Tricolator, a company that specialized in combining a piece such as this one with a warmer base, a metal frame, etc. It was common practice for a pottery company to make items such as this to fill a special order — not just for Tricolator but for similar companies as well. You can also find coffeepots that were made for Tricolator by Hall, some of which bear the marks of both companies. These bowls have been reported in ivory, yellow, red, turquoise, and green; cobalt may also exist. When found, they're normally open, though one collector tells us his was bought at an estate sale topped with the standard Fiesta casserole lid.

Plate 9

22

Plate 10

Plate 11

Plate 12

Plate 13

This is the unlisted salad bowl; it's very rare in cobalt as well as ivory and red.

Plate 14

Bulb Candle Holders. Both these and the tripod candle holders were original; this style was discontinued sometime between 1944 and late 1946. They are found in the six early colors and are relatively easy to find.

Plate 15

Tripod Candle Holders. These are regarded as very desirable additions to any collection. They're scarce and are found in only the first six colors, since they were discontinued around 1942 or '43.

Plate 16

Carafe. The carafe was an original item but was no longer listed by 1946. The stopper has a cork seal, and its unique shape makes it a favorite among collectors. (It was a turquoise carafe that captivated us first. We bought it for a friend who, knowing our passion for flea markets, asked us to pick up Fiesta for her to add to the set she'd received for her wedding. This was the only piece we ever gave her, and we hated to part with it.) You'll find it in the first six colors with red and ivory most scarce. The company lists its capacity as three pints.

Plate 17

This demitasse pot was originally Fiesta red (see interior color) but now is glazed in a copper-bronze luster, and we know of another with silver over its original green. Their decorator remains a mystery. If you're lucky enough to find a similar one, expect to pay at least double the going rate for red. Another pot has been reported in a rich burgundy wine.

Plate 13

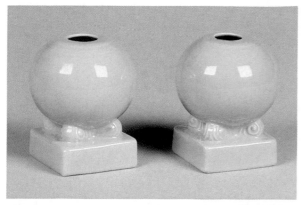

Plate 14

Plate 15

Plate 16

Plate 18

Teacups with the inside rings (right) are the oldest — these also have a hand-turned foot. Only a few of these have been found in medium green which would seem to indicate that it was sometime around 1959 when those with inside rings were discontinued. The teacup on the left represents the second style. Note that the third style (center back), though produced in the color assortment available through the sixties, has the 'C' handle of Fiesta Ironstone — evidently manufactured near the time of the restyling.

Plate 19

Demitasse Pot, Demitasse Cups and Saucers. Both the pot and cups were in the original line. The pot was dropped before 1944; you'll find it in the six original colors with red, turquoise, and ivory rather scarce. The cups and saucers were made in ten colors (no medium green, since they were discontinued in '56) with fifties colors hardest to find and selling at a premium. A collector once reported one in a brick-red glaze.

Plate 20

Coffeepot, Teacups and Saucers. The coffeepot can be found in all of Fiesta's colors except medium green. It was in the original line but was not made after mid-1956. Of course, teacups are always in demand. Though it is a rare occurrence, a few cups have been reported bearing the HLC inkstamp.

Plate 17

Plate 18

Plate 19

Plate 20

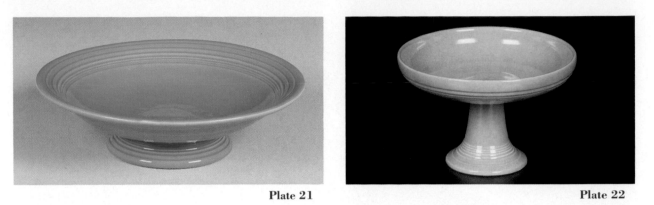

Plate 21   **Plate 22**

Plate 21
   Comport. These were made from 1936 until sometime between '44 and 1946; they're 12" in diameter and can be found in the six original colors.

Plate 22
   Sweets Comport. We found that the sweets compotes, though part of the original line, were discontinued between 1944 and 1946, so they are available only in the six early colors. These are 3½" tall, and only about one out of four examples is marked with the ink stamp.

Plate 23
   Marmalade (top**) and Mustard (**bottom**).** Marmalades and mustards were two of the items mentioned in Rhead's August 1936 magazine article quoted in the chapter entitled 'The Story of Fiesta.' He wrote that these were new to the line at that time. They were discontinued between 1944 and 1946, so they're found in the first six colors only.

Plate 24
   Egg Cup. From one of the newly-found price lists, we learned that the egg cup was not original but was added to the line in mid-'36. They were discontinued between January and September of 1956 and are available in ten colors (no medium green). Collectors report that chartreuse and gray are the hardest to find.

Plate 25
   Tom and Jerry Mug. These mugs, sometimes referred to as coffee mugs, have always been popular with collectors. They were also reported in Rhead's article (mid-'36) as new to the line and continued in production until the end. They were made in all eleven colors, though ivory ones are scarce. You'll find they often vary a little in height as well as in thickness, due to subtle changes in the molds that were used.

Plate 26
   Creamer and Sugar Bowl, Individual; Figure-8 Tray. This set is from the 1939–43 sales campaign. Nearly all sets are found with the sugar and creamer in yellow on a cobalt tray; however, occasionally you'll find a red creamer and once in awhile a turquoise or yellow tray. Though no more than two or three have been reported, creamers have been found in turquoise, and one sugar bowl is known to exist in this color. A cobalt creamer has been found by an advanced collector with many years' experience who is confident that it is old, due to the fact that the cobalt exactly matches the lighter tone of the original line and the gauge is thinner, not as thick as the new Fiesta.

Plate 27
   Creamer and Sugar Bowl. Shown here in red, the creamer (which collectors call the 'regular' creamer) replaced the original stick-handled variety in the Fall of 1939 and continued in production until restyled for the Ironstone line. The sugar bowl remained basically the same from '36 on, though the bases of earlier creamers and sugar bowls are flared out as compared to those made in the late forties in the original colors and those in the fifties colors, when a slight change in the molds resulted in a base with a rather stubby appearance.
   Stick-Handled Creamer. These were made from 1936 until late 1939 when they were replaced by the ring-handled style above. They come in the six early colors and are hardest to find in turquoise (as shown).

Plate 24

Plate 23

Plate 25

Plate 26

Plate 27

Plate 28

A sales promotion offered in 1952 is represented in Plate 28 — a gray pitcher along with a pair of tumblers in each of these colors: dark green, Harlequin yellow, and chartreuse. These are very hard to find. One collector's theory, and it may well be fact, is that this set was dipped to go with Rhythm. The dates coincide. He pointed out that a Fiesta juice set and mixing bowls in Jubilee colors had been used to promote Jubilee, and we know there are bowls in Rhythm colors — it makes perfect sense that a juice set might have been part of Rhythm's promotional campaign, too.

Plate 29

Juice pitchers in colors other than yellow and red are very rare. This one in turquoise, shown along-side its larger counterpart, is a one-of-a-kind example. Another has been reported in light green.

Plate 30

Disk Water Pitcher, Water Tumblers. Not original but added to the line in 1939, the disk water pitcher continued to be made until the end of production. It's very scarce in medium green and chartreuse and rather hard to find in the fifties colors. The tumblers were discontinued between '44 and '46 having been made since the onset of production; so they're found in the original six colors only with turquoise perhaps being a little scarce.

Plate 31

Disk Juice Pitcher, Juice Tumblers. Of all the promotional items, the 30-oz. juice pitcher and 5-oz. tumblers are the only ones that are easy to find. Nearly every pitcher you'll see will be yellow (collectors report a high incidence of the use of Harlequin yellow, a slightly brighter shade than Fiesta yellow), though on rare occasions you may find one in red. Though juice tumblers were discontinued before the fifties, rose tumblers are not uncommon. Rose was a standard Harlequin color in the late '30s and was 'borrowed' to add a seventh color to the seven-piece juice set.

Plate 28

Plate 29

Plate 30

Plate 31

Plate 32

Relish Tray. Five individual sections fit into the base of the relish tray. Its round center is often mistaken for a coaster; and, although never produced with that use in mind, it seems likely that some may have been bought for that purpose since we have had several reports from collectors who have found groups of them in old estates. Color make-up is important in determining the value of a relish tray. Red or cobalt are the most desirable base colors; and the more sections present in these colors, the higher the price.

2-Pint Jug. The 2-pint jug (shown here in gray) was part of the original assortment. It was made until mid-'56, so it comes in all colors but medium green.

Ice Pitcher. Made from 1936 until sometime between 1944 and '46 in the original colors only, the ice pitcher is a little hard to find in ivory, but it's red that tops the price scale. Though is looks seem to suggest otherwise, it does not take a lid. We have a photo in our file of an example in a mottled orange glaze similar to several items we saw in the morgue, but this one was found outside the plant by the collector who sent us the picture. Though we've always considered this glaze 'experimental,' we recently learned that a line with a very similar glaze was produced by Stangl. The orange mottle is used with cobalt and purple in the Stangl line, producing an effect reminiscent of patina on old copper, and the line has a Mediterranean flavor. Could HLC have made a similar line in a very limited amount? Perhaps.

Plate 33

Cake Plate. The 10" cake plate is completely flat and very, very rare. We've never found it mentioned in any of the company's literature; but since it has been reported in all six original colors (one in ivory finally turned up), it has to be an early piece. One lucky collector's cake plate bears an original paper label that reads 'Cake Kraft.'

Plate 34

Deep Plate. The deep plate was an August 1936 item that continued in production until the restyling — it's 8¾" in diameter and is found in all eleven colors.

Plate 35

These two syrup bottoms provide the basis for a rather unlikely but true tale. The syrup is the only piece of Fiesta that Rhead did not design; and, considering the careful attention he paid to detail throughout the line, it seems strange that he did not alter it to at least include the band of rings. The mold was bought from the DripCut Company, who made the tops for HLC. The blue one is molded of white ceramic and is marked 'DripCut, Heatproof, L.A., Cal.' The red one is genuine Fiesta. Decades ago a tea company filled syrup bases with tea leaves, added a cork stopper and their label, and unwittingly contributed to the frustration of today's collectors who have only a bottom. (See chapter entitled 'Commercial Adaptations and Ephemera.')

Plate 36

This photo shows why the Ironstone sauce boat stand in red is so attractive to Fiesta collectors. The sauce boat shown here is from the old line, but no stand was available until the advent of Fiesta Ironstone in 1969.

Plate 32

Plate 33

Plate 34

Plate 37

Compartment Plate, 12". These were made from 1936 until mid-'37. They are not mentioned on the May 1937 price list and have never been found in turquoise. They're rather scarce; actual measurement is 11½".

Compartment Plate 10½". Not quite as scarce, this size replaced the larger one in mid-'37. It was dropped in 1956, three years before the advent of medium green. These measure very close to the listed size.

Chop Plate 15". Both chop plates were in the original assortment. This one was discontinued early in 1956, so it is found in all colors except medium green. Actual measurement is 14¼".

Chop Plate 13". This size continued to be made until the restyling and can be found in all eleven colors. A black example was reported several years ago — well before the new black Fiesta was conceived. These actually measure 12¼".

Plates, 10", 9", 7", 6". Plates have always been in good supply, however the 10" size is fast becoming less than abundant. The number of rings within the foot area on the back of any Fiesta plate will vary; these identified the particular jigging machine that made it and were used in quality control. Occasionally you may notice when you stack your plates that not all are the same depth. If there was a reason or a purpose for this variation, we are not aware of it. From the 10" down to the 6" size, they're available in all eleven colors. They actually measure 10⅜", 9½", 7½", and 6½".

Plate 38

Sauce Boat. The sauce boat (gravy boat) was produced from 1937 until 1973 in all of Fiesta's colors with red and the colors of the fifties the most difficult to find.

Platter. The platter was first listed in July 1938 and continued in production until the restyling (Fiesta Ironstone) when it was enlarged to 13". It is easy to find in all eleven colors; it measures 12½".

Utility Tray. Added to the line in mid-'36, the utility tray (referred to as 'celery tray' on Western price lists) continued in production until sometime between '44 and '46, so you'll find them in only the first six colors with red perhaps a bit hard to find.

Syrup. Syrups rate very high with collectors. You'll find them in only the first six colors. They're scarce in ivory.

Salt and Pepper Shakers. These were made during the entire production period and can be found in all the Fiesta colors. Aside from the larger Kitchen Kraft shakers, this is the only style made in Fiesta. You may find a good imitation with holes on the side, but they are not genuine. Remember that Fiesta was widely copied, not only the bright glazes but often the band of rings as well. As a collector recently pointed out, Amberstone and Ironstone shakers do not have a center hole and she has seen yellow and medium green shakers with no center hole as well.

Plate 35

Plate 36

Plate 37

Plate 38

Plate 39

Handled Chop Plate. This is how this plate was referred to in the '39–'43 selling campaign. It was offered along with seven other items at the very attractive price of $1.00. The rattan-wrapped handles were of course manufactured by another company and shipped to HLC where they were fitted to these plates. They have been found in sizes to fit the 7", 9", and 10" plates (this size also fits the relish tray) as well as the 13" and 15" chop plates.

Plate 40

Teapot, Large. This was in the original assortment. It was made only until sometime between '44 and '46, so it's found in just the first six colors.

Teapot, Medium. This size was added to the line in 1937 and was available throughout the entire production period. You'll find it in all eleven colors.

Have you ever seen the look-alike child's tea set from Japan? The teapot and creamer are very accurate in every respect, but the sugar bowl has the ring handles instead of the scrolled tab handles of the genuine article. It comes with six cups and saucers, and it's fantastic!

Plate 41

Bud Vase. Part of the original line, the bud vase was discontinued between '44 and '46. It's fairly easy to find and was made in the first six colors. An unusual example in black was reported several years ago (not from the new line), and you may find a very similar design by Van Briggle. HLC's is 6¼" tall.

Flower Vase, 8". All three sizes of the flower vases were introduced in mid-'36 according to Rhead's magazine article. They're all very scarce and valued highly by collectors. This size continued longest in production — it was dropped between '44 and '46.

Flower Vase, 10". This size was made only from mid-'36 until Fall of 1942. Of the three, this one seems to be the most scarce.

Flower Vase, 12". This size was discontinued at the same time as the 10" vase. All are available in only the first six colors. One of our fondest memories is a visit to East Liverpool when we were beginning to research the first Fiesta book. We found a little antique store well stocked with good Fiesta; among several other purchases we took home a pair of 12" vases in cobalt at $7.00 each.

Plate 39

Plate 40

Plate 41

Plate 42

38

We thought you'd enjoy seeing this full-page shot of some nice medium green items. This color has become scarce and is considered very desirable by collectors today. Some pieces of Fiesta are very rare in medium green, for instance: the deep plate, cream soup, 6" bowl, 4¾" fruit, disk pitcher, casserole, and medium teapot. And, of course, since it was not introduced until '59 and many pieces had been discontinued by then, some items are simply not available in this color. Even to the most experienced eye, the difference between a heavy application of light green and the average in medium green is sometimes a bit tricky to discern. Over the past few years we've had may newcomers who have asked for some help in sorting out all those greens. We hope that the shaker photo (Plate 43) will visually 'fill the bill.' The medium green shaker is in the foreground, the light green to the left, the dark green at the top, and the chartreuse to the right.

Plate 43

FIESTA IRONSTONE

In 1969 Fiesta was restyled, and the line that was offered in February of the following year was called Fiesta Ironstone. There were many factors that of necessity brought this change about. Labor and production costs had risen sharply. Efforts to hold these costs down resulted in the use of two new colors which were standard colors for several other lines of dinnerware produced at HLC: Antique Gold and Turf Green. This eliminated the need of the separate firing that had been necessary for the older Fiesta colors. It was pointed out to us as we toured the factory that since each color required different temperatures in the kiln, orders were running ahead of production for Fiesta as well as their other lines. In order to cut labor cost, all markings were eliminated. (You will very seldom find an item with the Fiesta stamp; this was never the practice, and such pieces must be from early in the transition.)

The restyled pieces had a more contemporary feeling — bowls were flared, and the applied handles were only partial rings. The covered casserole had molded, closed handles, and the handles had been eliminated entirely from the sugar bowl. The covered coffee server made a return appearance after an absence of several years. Twenty-two items were offered in three colors: Antique Gold, Turf Green, and the original red, now called Mango Red. The oval platter was enlarged from 12" to 13"; three new items were offered, the soup/cereal, the sauce boat stand, and the 10" salad bowl.

Finally in November 1972, all production of Fiesta red was discontinued because many of the original technicians who developed this color and maintained control over the complicated manufacturing and firing had retired, and modern mass-production methods were unsuited to the process. On January 1, 1973, the famous line of Fiesta dinnerware was discontinued altogether.

Because Ironstone was made for a relatively short time, it is not easy to find. But since the old Fiesta line has become so costly to collect, enthusiasm for the Ironstone has recently begun to generate. Red mugs and the sauce boat stand in any color are regarded as 'good pieces.' Red is the most difficult color to find; green is scarce in some pieces, gold is the most available, and that's the only color many of the larger items were ever made in. You may find cups with the Ironstone handle in Fiesta yellow, medium green, and turquoise. (For a complete listing of available items, see 'Suggested Values' in the back of the book.)

Plate 44

FIESTA KITCHEN KRAFT

Since the early 1930s, the Homer Laughlin China Company had been well known as manufacturers of a wide variety of ceramic kitchenwares. In 1939 they introduced a bake-and-serve line called Fiesta Kitchen Kraft as an extension of their already popular genuine Fiesta ware. This they offered in four original Fiesta colors — red, yellow, green, and blue. The following pieces (compiled from the April 1941 price list) were available:

Covered jars: small, medium, and large
Mixing bowls: 10", 8", and 6"
Covered casseroles: 8½", 7½", and individual
Pie plate, 10"
Salt and pepper shakers, large

Covered jug, large
Spoon, fork, and cake server
Refrigerator set, 4-pc.
Cake plate, 11"
Plates: 6" and 9"

These were chosen from the standard assortment of kitchenware items which had been the basis of the many Kitchen Kraft and Oven-Serve decaled lines of years previous; none were created especially for Fiesta Kitchen Kraft. This line was in production for a relatively short period — perhaps being discontinued sometime during WWII prior to 1945.

In addition to the items listed previously, there are at least three more to add. These may have been offered in the original assortment and discontinued by the 1941 listing. They are: the oval platter in a chrome holder (which was shipped as a unit from HLC), a 9" pie plate, and a variation in size of the covered jug. The difference is so slight, even side by side it could go unnoticed. Collectors report as many of one size as the other. If you really want to label yours large or small, check the circumference. The larger one measures 21½" while the smaller one is 20".

The 6" and 9" plates listed on the 1941 illustrated brochure were used as underplates for the casseroles. When we visited the morgue at HLC, we saw an example of these. They were of a thinner gauge and seemed to have been taken from one of their other lines, since the style was not typical. They were round and had a moderately wide, slightly flared rim. Although none have been reported in Fiesta KK colors, there is one in ivory with decals shown in the chapter 'Kitchen Kraft and Oven-Serve.'

If you have been interested at all in the decaled lines, you are probably familiar enough with the Kitchen Kraft molds that you recognize them easily. Several collectors have mentioned finding their stack set, salt and peppers, mixing bowls, and other items in an ivory glaze; but as far as we can determine from any information available, ivory was never listed as a Fiesta Kitchen Kraft color; so these are rare. Of the four standard colors, dark blue is most in demand and along with red represents the high side of the price range.

Trademarks:

Plate 47
   Mixing Bowls. The mixing bowls measure 10", 8", and 6" and have proven to be rather difficult to find. Note the original sticker on the large one. They have been found in white as well as Harlequin, Jubilee, and Rhythm colors. Such bowls may or may not be marked. Although a kitchenware bowl seems an unlikely liquor decanter, the 6" size has been reported with this message in gold underglaze lettering: 'This whiskey is 4 years old, 90 proof Maryland straight rye whiskey, Wm. Jameson, Inc., N.Y., Shorewood, the finest name in rye.'

Plate 48
   Casseroles. These come in three sizes: 8½", 7½", and individual. All are scarce; the small one is especially attractive to collectors, and they are usually high in price. Plate 45 shows lid detail.

Plate 49
   Covered Jars. To determine the size of your covered jar, measure the circumference. The large jar is 27½" around, the medium 22", and the small one is 14¼". These make lovely (though unhandy) canisters in a vintage kitchen. Lid detail is evident in Plate 46.

Plate 45

Plate 46

Plate 47

Plate 48

Plate 49

Plate 51

Covered Jug. There are two sizes in these jugs, but the differences are subtle. The circumference of the larger is 21½"; the smaller measures 20" around.

Stack Set (Refrigerator Jars). The covered refrigerator stack set consists of three units and a flat lid and are usually made up of all four Kitchen Kraft colors. A rare few components have been found in the ivory line. No, trust me — these are not dog dishes.

Plate 52

Cake Plate. These may or may not be marked. The only decoration is the narrow band around the edge formed by one inverted ring. They are much easier to find than the regular Fiesta cake plate.

Pie Plates. These come in two sizes: 10" and 9". Actually they measure 10¼" and 9¾" (read the chapter 'Dating Codes and English Measurements' if you're as confused as we once were). They were produced without rings either inside or outside and are usually not marked, though we have one with a gold Fiesta stamp. The 10" size has been reported in the maroon and spruce green of the Harlequin line (see Plate 56). In the chapter called 'Go-Alongs,' you'll see the metal frame (similar to the one in Plate 54) that was sometimes shipped along with the pie plates directly from the factory. It is very unusual to find the small size in the Fiesta KK colors; it is more often found in ivory decorated with decals.

Plate 53

Servers: Spoon, Cake Lifter, Fork. These are all rated highly by collectors and are not easily found. Their handles are decorated with the same embossed flowers as one of the Oven-Serve lines. Plate 50 shows the completed collection displayed to full advantage. There's another spoon, about 1" longer and slightly narrower, though they're very rare. We've seen it in ivory, and one of our survey collectors reports an example with decals, knows of two in ivory, and another in turquoise, which he says came from the Well's estate. He has seen a brochure from Homer Laughlin that shows a light green one, and says that a collector in Ohio may have a fork and pie server in a size that corresponds.

Salt and Pepper Shakers. These are larger replicas of their Fiesta dinnerware counterparts, although by no means as plentiful. You may on rare occasions find them glazed in Harlequin yellow.

Plate 50

Plate 51

Plate 52

Plate 53

Plate 54

Platter. This is the 13" oval platter, shown in Harlequin spruce green, not a Fiesta Kitchen Kraft color. These are very, very rare in this color. A few have been found in Harlequin yellow, and one has been reported in mauve blue. Even in the regular four Fiesta Kitchen Kraft colors, these are scarce. They're not usually marked. The metal holder is an HLC issue, though of course not all were sold in a frame.

Plate 55

This stack set has lots going for it — a unit and a lid in ivory and an original Kitchen Kraft sticker as well.

Plate 56

This red lid fits the stacking units perfectly, and that's about all we *do* know about it. It may even have been made for some other purpose — a hot plate, for instance, for the regular Fiesta line (the band of rings does seem out of step in Kitchen Kraft). To our knowledge, this is the only one ever found.

Plate 57

Here's a couple of very unusual pie plates. The 9" plate is trimmed in gold and stamped with an advertising message; the larger plate has been dipped in Harlequin spruce green.

Plate 54

Plate 55 **Plate 56** **Plate 57**

THE FIESTA CASUALS

GENUINE

fiesta

H. L. Co. USA
CASUAL

There were two designs produced in the beautiful Fiesta Casuals; and, although they are both relatively difficult to find, often when they are found the set may be complete, or nearly so. They were introduced in June 1962; and as sales were only moderately active, they were discontinued around 1968. The Plaid Stamp Company featured both lines in their illustrated catalogs during these years.

The Hawaiian 12-Point Daisy design featured a ½" turquoise band at the rim and turquoise daisies with brown centers on a white background. The other pattern was Yellow Carnation which featured the yellow flowers with a touch of brown on white background. A yellow rim band completed the design. In each line, only the dinner plates, salad plates, saucers, and oval platters were decorated; the cups, fruit dishes, nappies, sugar bowls, and creamers were simply glazed in the matching Fiesta color. The designs were hand sprayed and overglazed using a lead mask with the cut-out motif. A complete service consisted of six place settings: dinner plate, salad plate, cup and saucer, and 5½" fruit. A platter, 8½" nappy, and the sugar and creamer were also included. (For a listing of available items, see 'Suggested Values' in back of book.)

Plate 58

47

Plate 59

Plate 60

FIESTA WITH STRIPES

We have no information concerning the decorator of this line of striped Fiesta; but it must have been done sometime between 1944 and 1946 since, in addition to the items shown, a fruit compote, footed salad bowl, and bulb and tripod candle holders have also been found. Several of these pieces were discontinued at that time. So far, only red and blue stripes have been reported. This dinnerware is very rare. The stripes are under the glaze and are resistant to wear; you may find some plates with overglaze stripes (one at the rim and another inside the band of rings) that are usually very worn. These have little value. (Photography © Adam Anik.)

Plate 61

FIESTA WITH DECALS

Here and on the following pages are examples of Fiesta with decals. You'll find other examples not shown. They may have been decorated by HLC, but more than likely the work was done by smaller decorating companies — there were several in the immediate vicinity. We are sure that the turkey plates shown in Plate 62 were done by Homer Laughlin. According to the company, commercial grade ware was used for this line. These are rare. Shown is the 9" plate with a maroon band, a 13" chop plate with a yellow band, and the Kitchen Kraft cake plate trimmed in gold. The 15" chop plate has also been reported with the turkey decal.

Plate 62

Plate 63

The floral dinnerware in Plate 63 is only one example — you'll find various decals, and some may be trimmed with bands or stripes around the rims. The cake sets in Plate 64 are backstamped Royal China. They are decorated with eighteenth-century garden scenes and gold work, and each set consists of the 15" chop plate and six matching plates. In previous editions we have shown the same decoration on shapes other than Fiesta; those were marked 'Georgian by Homer Laughlin, Royal China.' Plate 65 shows another example, this time it's an A.D. cup and saucer; the decal is one that is also used in the cake set described above. These were done by Royal China as well.

More often than not, examples with decal decoration are in ivory. This makes the yellow and cobalt relish tray in Plate 66 especially nice. Shown in Plate 67, a set of two red cups and saucers presented to Mother and Father on the occasion of their 35th anniversary in 1936, the year Fiesta was introduced.

Plate 64

Plate 65

Plate 66

Tom and Jerry mugs and a footed salad bowl in ivory (Plate 68) were trimmed with gold bands and lettering to make a T&J set that is very hard to find complete; bowls are more difficult to locate than mugs. HLC issued a calendar plate for a number of years, using whatever blanks were available. In 1954 and 1955, they just happened to use Fiesta, see Plate 69. The 9" plate in the center is the rare size; it may be found for either year. The 1954 plate has been found in ivory only, the '55 may be green, yellow, or ivory. The bud vase (Plate 70) is hand-painted, rather than decaled, and the decorator is unknown.

Plate 67

Plate 68

Plate 70

Plate 69

NEW FIESTA

After a 13-year absence, Fiesta was reintroduced to the market on February 28th, 1986. Just a short time before that, several lines of colored dinnerware had been introduced by competitors — among them Moderna by Mikasa and a line-for-line interpretation of Fiesta by Rego China, made for the restaurant trade. These were enjoying enough success to convince Homer Laughlin to test the waters. Sample items were produced and dipped in a number of colors to test market preferences at a Chicago trade show in December 1985. A gray and yellow was also tested in addition to the five winning colors of Cobalt Blue (darker and denser than the original), Rose (a true pink), White, Apricot (a pale peach), and Black. Interest was great enough to begin production. A last minute decision to go with a vitrified body (as opposed to the semi-vitrified clay used for the original Fiesta) was made to appeal to the restaurant trade. While vitrified china is denser and will not absorb moisture, it has to be fired at a higher temperature. Because of this, some shapes had a tendency to deform. Thus the Ironstone-style casserole, sugar bowl, coffee sever, and flat teapot lid had to be redesigned. The original brochures used photographs of the semi-vitrified samples and showed the Ironstone-style handled casserole. But this particular item was never produced in the new line; instead it was restyled into the covered casserole shown in Plate 71. The coffee server was replaced by the restyled version (see plate 73 for both styles, the restyle is in the foreground), and the sugar bowl was replaced with one made from the old marmalade mold (without the notch for the spoon) in the first few months of production.

Several colors have been added since the introduction — Turquoise (darker, with more of a green cast than the old color), Yellow (very pale), Periwinkle Blue (pastel gray-blue), and Seamist Green (pale mint green, added in spring 1991). A limited line in Lilac (rich and deep-toned) became available early in 1994; not all accessory shapes were produced, though, and it was to be made for only two years. In the summer of 1995, the last new color, Persimmon, made its debut at the first national Fiesta collectors' convention, 'Fiesta Alive in '95,' in Kansas City, Missouri. The new color is a hot and heady reddish-coral tone, and Persimmon seems to be a well-chosen name. This color was developed exclusively for sale through Bloomingdale's. The company has stated its intention to phase out Cobalt and Black; but, as a company official explained, it can take up to five years to discontinue a color. Major catalog houses and restaurant supply companies require open stock agreements, and a line or color cannot be discontinued overnight, thus Black and Cobalt have been designated special order colors by HLC and are not being carried in stock.

Plate 71

A number of items have been added to the line since 1986, many of them designed for the restaurant trade. In addition to the items shown in the catalog page line drawing, a 9" rimmed soup, a 12" rimmed bowl, and a 13¼" platter were introduced in the Fall of 1990. The items marked with an asterisk were added to the line in time for our 1994 update; those with two asterisks have been added since then.

Covered Butter Dish*
Covered Teapot
9½" Oval Platter*
Medium Flower Vase, 9½"
Small Disk Pitcher
9" Luncheon Plate*
Saucer
Coffee Server
Regular Covered Sugar
4" Bouillon Cup*
After Dinner Coffee Cup
 and Saucer**
9" Rimmed Soup Bowl**
Napkin Rings**

Salt and Pepper
32-Oz. Serving Bowl
Covered Casserole
12" Chop Plate
Large Disk Pitcher
7⅛" Salad Plate
Cup
Bulb Candle Holders
Regular Creamer
5½" Cereal Bowl*
Cake Plate/Serving
 Tray, 11"**
12" Centerpiece Bowl**

Sugar and Creamer on Figure-8 Tray
11½" Oval Platter*
Sauce Boat
Bud Vase
10½" Dinner Plate
6½" Bread and Butter Plate*
10-oz. Coffee Mug*
Pyramid (tripod) Candle Holders
5¼" Fruit Bowl*
6⅞" Soup/Cereal Bowl
Miniature Disk Picture, 3"**
13½" Oval Platter**
Table Lamp (J.C. Penney exclusive,
 spring 1993)

And there may be other items as well.

All of the above pieces are marked (including cups) with the exception of the butter dish. The cast-indented mark is very similar to the old; the ink-stamped items are marked with a new version (see line drawing).

In 1994 a line of new Fiesta decorated with Looney Tunes characters was marketed through Time-Warner Outlet Stores. It will probably become very collectible, and we wanted to make you aware of it. The line consists of only a few items: cup and saucer, 10" dinner plate, fruit bowl, soup bowl, pie baker, teapot, creamer and sugar bowl on the figure-eight tray, and the disk pitcher. Colors in use are Rose, Periwinkle Blue, Yellow, and Turquoise.

GENUINE

Fiesta

H•L•Co

U.S.A.

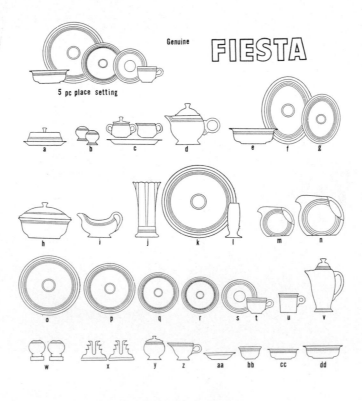

Genuine FIESTA

5 pc place setting

a b c d e f g

h i j k l m n

o p q r s t u v

w x y z aa bb cc dd

Plate 72

Plate 73

Plate 74

Plate 75

Plate 76

Because there was so much variation in the old turquoise shade, the new turquoise is the only color likely to cause any confusion and then only when it is not compared to an old piece. Almost all the new items will be slightly smaller and heavier than the old, due to the vitrified clay. In addition, all new items will have a 'wiped' versus a glazed foot (the new items sit directly on the kiln shelves, and so cannot be glazed on the contact points). If an item has three sagger pin marks, it is almost certainly old.

In addition to the regular Fiesta line (which is targeted toward the general public), several items were produced to appeal specifically to the collector market. Prior to the reintroduction of Fiesta, Homer Laughlin produced a limited edition Commemorative Fiesta 50th Anniversary Collector's Mug set for a private company, China Specialties, Inc. Less than six hundred sets were produced, each consisting of ten white mugs decorated with the Fiesta Dancing Senorita Trademark in a Fiesta color (red, yellow, cobalt, turquoise, light green, forest green, rose, chartreuse, gray, and medium green). Later, Homer Laughlin also brought out a collector/dealer sign for Fiesta, a 12" white chop plate with the Fiesta logo in Mango Red. A relative few were produced in yellow and apricot with the Mango Red decoration.This piece is shown on the right in Plate 75; the one on the far left was produced by HLC for their dealers — it shows their new logo. In 1987 Homer Laughlin decided to try a Christmas line featuring Fiesta. White Fiesta was decorated with a green holly decal and red piping at the rim. The line was not a huge success for most retailers and was produced for the 1987 Christmas season only. While it has not been produced since, HLC has not officially retired Holiday Fiesta from its catalog, and it might be reintroduced at some point in the future.

We want to thank Joel Wilson (China Specialties) for this New Fiesta rewrite and for supplying us with items for our photographs.

HARLEQUIN

Harlequin was produced by Homer Laughlin in an effort to serve all markets and to fit every budget. It was a less expensive dinnerware and was sold without trademark through the F. W. Woolworth Company exclusively. The following is an excerpt from one of the company's original illustrated brochures:

> The new Harlequin Pottery offers a gift to table gaiety. It brings the magic of bright, exciting color to the table, dresses the festive board with pleasantness and personality, makes of every meal a cheerful and companionable occasion.
>
> The new ware comes in four lovely colors . . . Yellow, Green, Red, and Blue . . . and offers the hostess endless possibilities for creating interesting and appealing color effects on her table. All the colors are brilliant and eye-catching . . . designed to go together effectively in any combination the hostess may desire. To set a table with Harlequin is an adventure in decoration. Plates are of one color, cups of another, saucers and platters of another . . . you can give free range to your artistic instincts.
>
> And it is very easy to build up a comprehensive set of Harlequin in whatever items and colors you desire, because it may be bought by the piece at extremely reasonable prices.
>
> Sold Exclusively by
> F. W. WOOLWORTH CO. STORES

Although it was first listed on company records as early as 1936, Harlequin was not actively introduced to the public until 1938.

It was designed by Fredrick Rhead, and like Fiesta the style was pure Art Deco. Rhead again used the band of rings device as its only ornamentation, but this time chose to space the rings well away from the rim. Flat pieces were round and concave with the center areas left plain. Hollowware pieces were cone shaped; bowls were flared. Handles were applied with small ornaments at their bases and, with few exceptions, were extremely angular.

Over the years the color assortment grew to include all of Fiesta's lovely colors with the exceptions of ivory and dark blue. The original colors (those mentioned in the brochure we just quoted), however, were developed just for Harlequin. Harlequin yellow was a lighter and brighter tint than Fiesta yellow; the green was a spruce green, and the blue tended toward a mauve shade. It is interesting to note that the color the company referred to as 'red' is actually maroon. To avoid confusion, today's collectors reserve 'red' for the orange-red color of Fiesta red.

It seems logical here to conclude that because Harlequin was not extensively promoted until 1938 that it would have been then or soon after that the line was expanded and new colors added. The new colors of the forties were red (orange-red like Fiesta's — called tangerine by the company), rose (though records show a color called salmon that preceded rose, if indeed these are two individual shades, the difference is so slight it is of no significance to today's collectors), turquoise, and light green. (There are some pieces whose production dates we can't pinpoint beyond the fact that they were not part of the original line but were listed as discontinued by 1952. Many of these are rarely if ever found in light green. This leads us to believe that light green may not have been added until the mid-forties.)

Gray, chartreuse, and forest (dark) green were new in the fifties. Harlequin yellow, turquoise, and rose continued to be produced. By 1959 the color assortment was reduced to four colors again — red (coinciding with the resumed production of Fiesta red), turquoise, Harlequin yellow, and the last new color, medium green.

The original line consisted of these items: 10", 9", 7", and 6" plates; 8" soup plate; 9" nappy; salt and pepper shakers; covered casserole; teacup and saucer; creamer, regular; sugar bowl; 11" platter; 5½" fruit; double egg cup; and 4½" tumbler.

These pieces were soon added to the original line: cream soup cup, sauce boat, after dinner cup and saucer, novelty creamer, 13" platter, teapot, syrup*, service water jug, 36s bowl, ash tray (both styles), 36s oatmeal, individual salad bowl, 22-oz. jug, 4½" tumbler, ash tray saucer*, basketweave nut dish*, relish tray with inserts*, individual egg cup*, individual creamer*, candle holders*, marmalade*, butter dish, tankard, and 9" baker. Of the assortment, those items marked with an asterisk (indicating them to be rare or non-existent in light green) were probably the first to be discontinued. Knowing that the Fiesta line suffered a severe pruning during 1944 – '45, it would certainly follow that the same fate would befall Harlequin.

The material available to us for study dated May 1952 indicates that even more pieces had by then been dropped: the 9" baker, the covered butter dish, the individual creamer, and the tankard.

Harlequin proved to be quite popular and sold very well into the late fifties when sales began to diminish. Records show that the final piece was actually manufactured in 1964.

In 1939 the Hamilton Ross Co. offered a Harlequin look-alike which they called Sevilla. It came in assorted solid colors, eight in all, with the same angular handles, similar style and decoration. The round platter was distinctive. It featured closed handles formed by the band of rings device which was allowed to sweep gradually outward to just past mid-point; no doubt you have seen an occasional piece.

In 1979 Homer Laughlin announced that they had been approached and would comply with a request from the F.W. Woolworth Company to reissue the Harlequin line, one of that company's all time bestsellers, as part of their 100th Anniversary celebration. The Harlequin Ironstone dinnerware they produced was a very limited line and is easily recognized. It was made in two original colors: yellow and turquoise; a medium green that was slightly different than the original; and a new shade, coral. The sugar bowl was restyled with closed handles and a solid finial. A round platter (the original was oval) in coral was included in the 45-pc. set which was comprised of only plates, salad plates, cereal/soups, cups and saucers, yellow sugar, turquoise creamer, and a round green vegetable bowl. The plates were backstamped Homer Laughlin (the old ones are not marked), and even the pieces made from authentic molds are easy to distinguish from the old Harlequin. Because many of the lovely colors of the original line and virtually none of its unique accessory pieces were reproduced, this late line has never been a threat to the investments of the many collectors who love Harlequin dinnerware. We have talked with several dealers who actually felt the reissue stimulated interest in the old line.

A letter from the company dated April 1983 advised that Woolworth's as well as a few other dealers throughout the country were carrying the new Harlequin. It stated that a few round platters and vegetable bowls had been made in yellow by mistake, and that some of these were backstamped 'through error in the Dipping Department.' (These are shown in Plate 78 along with a white (a non-standard color) plate backstamped 1980 and a saucer, which should have been unmarked, backstamped 1982.) Production continued for no more than a couple of years; and, compared to the old line, sales were much more limited.

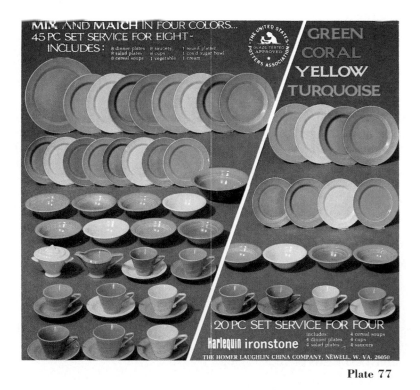

Plate 77

Plate 78

Plate 79

Mixing Bowls. These are the Kitchen Kraft bowls — the original owner bought them from the factory by mail order for $2.05 plus postage ($1.00 for the 10", 65¢ for the 8", and 40¢ for the 6"). They are unmarked. The set was also available with the smallest bowl in red for an additional 20¢.

Plate 80

Basketweave Ash Tray (left front). None of the ash trays were in the original assortment, but all were added very early — possibly even before 1940. The basketweave version may be found in all twelve colors including medium green.

Ash Tray Saucer (center). This is an unusual item; note the cigarette rest. These are hard to find; and because none have been reported in the fifties colors, medium green, or light green, they were probably discontinued in the mid-forties. A rare few have been reported in ivory — not a standard Harlequin color (though we know of an ivory tumbler as well).

Regular Ash Tray. So dubbed by collectors to make a distinction between the three types, this one comes in the first eight colors only. It's scarce in light green.

Plate 81

Cream Soup Bowl. This piece can be found in all colors; it's scarce in light green and very rare in medium green.

Plate 82

Oval Baker. Discontinued before the fifties colors were introduced, the oval baker is found in the first eight colors only. (Remember, though rose was a fifties color in Fiesta, it was introduced to the Harlequin line soon after 1938.) This piece is 9" long.

Plate 83

36s Oatmeal Bowl (far left). Shown here in light green, the 36s oatmeal measures 6½" in diameter. See the chapter entitled 'Dating Codes and English Measurements' for an explanation of the term '36s.'

Nappy (center back). The nappy, shown in spruce green, was part of the original line and can be found in all colors, although it is rare in medium green. It's 9" in diameter.

Individual Salad Bowl (right back). The individual salad is not so hard to find in the fifties colors; but both it and the 36s bowl are scarce in red, maroon, spruce green, and medium green.

36s Bowl (far right). Shown in a hard-to-find color, medium green, the 36s bowl was evidently not made much later than 1959 when this color was added to the line.

Fruit Bowl, 5½" (center front). This bowl has also been found in a slightly larger version that measures 6" across in maroon, blue, spruce green, and yellow.

Plate 79

Plate 80

Plate 81

Plate 82

Plate 83

Plate 84

Casserole. These are scarce in fifties colors, and so far none have been reported in medium green. As a general rule, you'll find much less medium green, chartreuse, gray, and dark green in Harlequin than in Fiesta.

Plate 85

Demitasse Coffee Cup and Saucer. The little demitasses have become scarce in the fifties colors and are very rare in medium green. They don't appear on the 1959 listing when medium green was introduced, so they couldn't have been made in any large quantity in that color.

Large Cup. In the past we have called the larger cup the 'tankard' simply because a tankard was found listed as discontinued before 1952, and this was the only piece of Harlequin we didn't have a name for. However, as a dedicated Harlequin collector has pointed out, since this item has been found in only the later color assortment (chartreuse, forest green, medium green, rose, turquoise, and yellow) and not at all in the colors that were dropped early, it was obviously not discontinued before '52 and is therefore not our 'tankard.' But we now believe that the fifties colors were introduced in the fall of 1951, so if this were the tankard, as another collector suggests may yet be the case, the fact that it was discontinued by 1952 would explain why it is so rare. But this line of reasoning has a couple of flaws! I have one in medium green, a 1959 color, and though the handle is typically angular like Harlequin, the body of these cups are the same shape as the Epicure cups from the mid-fifties! Can anyone solve the mystery?

Plate 86

Butter Dish, ½-Lb. Originally a Jade/Century piece, this butter dish was later glazed in Harlequin and Riviera colors and sold with both lines. They have been found in these colors: cobalt blue, rose, mauve blue, spruce green, light green, maroon, turquoise, red, ivory, and Fiesta and Harlequin yellows. (For more information on the origin of the butter dish, see Plate 159.)

Plate 87

Candle Holders. These were once thought non-existent in light green, but in the past few years a pair has been reported. Far from plentiful in any color, they were made in the first eight colors only.

Plate 88

High-Lip Creamer (top row). The 'high-lip' creamer is found in the four original colors only. Note the difference in the length of the lips on the two shown. The fact that they were trimmed by hand doesn't wholly explain the difference, since only these two variations have been reported. Evidently the style was deliberately changed at some point.

Individual Creamer (top right). You'll find this tiny pitcher only in the first eight colors. They're really not at all difficult to find, but they are scarce in light green.

Regular Creamer (bottom row). This item is available in all twelve colors.

Sugar Bowl. One collector reports that upon comparing several sugar bowls in his collection he suspects that those with the inside rings were earlier and that these rings were eliminated sometime during the forties.

Novelty Creamer. You can expect to find these in all colors. Though they're virtually non-existent in medium green, we have finally heard from a collector who does have one.

Plate 84

Plate 85

Plate 86

Plate 87

Plate 88

Plate 90

Marmalade. Found in the first eight colors only. Light green marmalades are very rare.

Nut Dish. The small basketweave nut dishes are found in the first eight colors — light green is quite rare. They were copied from a style imported from Japan which is identical except that the original is decorated with tiny multicolor flowers.

Individual Egg Cup. Though fairly common in yellow (shown), spruce green, mauve blue, maroon, turquoise, rose, and red, they're very rare in light green.

Double Egg Cup. This egg cup will hold an egg in both the top and bottom — the boiled egg in the smaller end, a poached egg in the larger (the idea being, we were told, to dunk toast triangles into the soft egg yolk). They're found in all twelve colors, but only four have been reported in medium green.

Perfume Bottle. These are not a standard part of the Harlequin line but are of interest to Harlequin collectors since they were dipped in Harlequin glazes. They're very hard to find.

Plate 91

Tumblers. These were discontinued before the fifties colors were introduced, so they're found in only the first eight colors. (Remember, though rose was a strictly a fifties color in the Fiesta line, it was made in Harlequin from the late thirties until late in the fifties; so don't be surprised to find a rose example, even though we don't show one here.) Collector friends of ours have one in ivory, not a standard Harlequin color. In Plate 89, the tumbler with the decal of an antique car is one of a set that was decorated by Pearl China.

Service Water Pitcher. Look for the Fiesta-like band of rings near the base on the water jug. This will help you identify the Harlequin jug from several look-alikes by other companies. It was produced in all twelve colors with medium green, gray, and dark green all very scarce. Just one has been reported in Fiesta yellow. We recently saw one of these etched 'Treasure Island, 1939.'

Plate 92

Salt and Pepper Shakers. These are easy to find. They were made in all of Harlequin's colors but are hard to find in medium green.

Jug, 22-Oz. These are commonly found in the first eleven colors; they're extremely rare in medium green.

Deep Plate. These can be found in all twelve colors; they measure 8" in diameter.

Sauce Boat. These are fairly easy to find in any of the twelve Harlequin colors.

Plate 89

Plate 90

Plate 91

Plate 92

Plate 93

   Plates, 10", 9", 7", 6". The 10" dinner plate is becoming very hard to find; the 9" and 7" have been reported in ivory, not a standard Harlequin color.
   Platters, 10", 13". These are generally easy to find in all twelve colors, though the smaller one is rare in medium green.

Plate 94

   Relish Tray. As strange as it seems, the true Harlequin relish tray base is found only in turquoise; these pie-wedge inserts are occasionally found in bases of another color, but those bases are actually Fiesta. The inserts are found in only seven of the first eight colors — no light green. The color combination as shown is the most common, but other combinations have also been reported. Two examples with all rose inserts have been found. Harlequin relish trays are rare and may on occasion come with a metal handle (see section on accessories and go-alongs).

Plate 95

   Syrup. Syrups are scarce and have been reported in only red, yellow, mauve, blue, spruce green, turquoise, light green, and ivory (and just one in each of the last three colors). Harlequin syrups are much rarer than their Fiesta counterparts.

Plate 96

   Teacups and Saucers. These are relatively easy to find in all twelve colors. One has been reported in a non-standard shade, Skytone Blue.
   Teapot. Teapots were made in all twelve colors but are hard to find in medium green.

Plate 93

Plate 94

Plate 95

Plate 96

HARLEQUIN ANIMALS

During the late thirties and early forties when miniatures such as these were enjoying a hey-day, HLC produced this menagerie as a part of the Harlequin line. There are six, each produced in four colors: maroon, spruce green, mauve blue, and yellow. They were marketed primarily through Woolworth Company stores.

In plate 97 are the original Harlequin animals in authentic glazes. There are no others, although you may find some that are very similar. The duck has a twin, a perpetually hungry little gander — his head bent into a permanent feeding position; but he was made by the Brush Pottery Company. And although several collectors were almost sure their 2½" elephant belonged in the group, HLC disowned him. A donkey look-alike pulling a cart may make you wonder at first, but a closer examination will reveal an uncharacteristic lack of sharp detail, and some of these have been found to bear a 'California' mark.

Plate 98 displays the 'Maverick' animals, a most appropriate term adopted by collectors to indicate animals that have been glazed by someone outside the Homer Laughlin China Company. In rare cases, you may find one in a standard Harlequin color that has been completely covered with gold, or it may be simply gold trimmed. One company involved in decorating the animals was Kaulware of Chicago, who utilized an iridescent glaze and gold hand-painted trim. You will find salt and pepper shakers in a slightly smaller size, indicating that they were cast from molds made from the original animals.

Another company responsible for producing some of the Mavericks was founded by John Kass, who operated in the East Liverpool, Ohio, area. During the Depression after his retail business failed, Kass built a small pottery (which he later expanded), employed members of his family, and began to make novelty items — salt and pepper shakers, small animal figures (Mavericks among them), and cups and saucers. A descendant of Kass's explained that it was a common practice in those days for area potters to 'make each other's items, and no one took offense.' All Kass's work was done painstakingly by hand from the casting to the final decoration. Business increased in the 1940s; the old buildings were replaced with modern structures, and more people were employed. 'We made the Harlequin animals from the very beginning, ' she continues. ' For some reason the ducks and penguins were made right up into the 1950s.' The letter goes on to say that there were other companies in the area who also made these animals. You will find that some of these are considerably smaller than the Harlequin animals and made of a finer, more porcelain-like material. Though most will be white with gold trim, some may be in colors. We have a gold-trimmed cobalt cat; and, until you compare it with the genuine article, you can't be sure that it isn't authentic. These smaller animals are worth considerably less than Mavericks that are full size or nearly so.

Though probably not a production run, there are a few red cats being found, and a red duck and penguin has been reported (See Plate 99). But be alert for painted frauds. Collectors tell us of finding red animals whose color, feel, and weight were perfect; but, they say, the paint was chipping off. Plate 100 shows turquoise, light green, and cobalt blue animals borrowed from HLC for their portrait photo. These are from their archives — don't expect to find them on the market.

Plate 97

Plate 98

Plate 99

Plate 100

RIVIERA AND IVORY CENTURY

Riviera was introduced by HCL in 1938 and was sold exclusively by the Murphy Company. In contrast to Fiesta and Harlequin, the line was quite limited. It was unmarked, lighter in weight, and therefore less expensive. Only rarely will you find a piece with the Homer Laughlin gold stamp. Of the three colored dinnerware lines, it has the rather dubious distinction of being the only one which was not originally created as such. Its forerunner was a line called Century — an ivory line with a vellum glaze. Century shapes were also decorated with a wide variety of decals and were the bases of many lines such as Mexicana and Hacienda. An enterprising designer (Rhead, no doubt) applied the popular colored glazes to these shapes, and Riviera was born. Even the shakers were from another line. They were originally designed as Tango, which accounts for the six-section design in contrast to the square Riviera shape.

Riviera is in very short supply; and, much to the chagrin of Riviera collectors everywhere, mint condition pieces are very few indeed. Flat pieces were especially bad to chip — plates, platters, saucers, and undersides of lids; but when it is found with no chips, the glaze is nearly always in beautiful condition.

Colors are mauve blue, red, yellow, light green, and ivory. On rare occasions, dark blue pieces are found, evidently made for special color effects. Though the old price lists we've seen never show ivory as part of the Riviera line, we have heard from a collector who bought the 20-piece service for four in its original box, and ivory was included, but no red. He believes that ivory was used as a Riviera color in the 1940s, while red was discontinued. At any rate, collectors appreciate the effect of the ivory with their Riviera and value these items as worthwhile additions to their collections.

Records for this line are especially scanty; but as accurately and completely as possible, here is a listing of the items in the line as it was first introduced. Sizes have been translated from the English measurements listed by the company and in our previous editions to actual sizes to the nearest inch.

11" dish (platter)	13" dish (platter)	10" plate
9" plate	6" plate	Teacup and saucer
Fruit	9" baker (oval vegetable bowl)	Salt and pepper shakers
Covered casserole	8" deep plate	8" nappy
6" oatmeal	Tumbler (with handle)	Open jug
Teapot	Sauce boat	(also found with lid)
Creamer	Covered sugar	

We have also found 15" platters, a covered syrup pitcher, and two sizes of butter dishes — a half-pound and a quarter-pound. In addition, there is a juice set. The juice jugs are standard though scarce in yellow, unusual in red, and extremely rare in mauve blue.

Although it is uncertain just when Riviera was discontinued, it was sometime prior to 1950. Riviera is a challenge to collect, but you can be sure the effort will be worthwhile — just wait until you see our new color photos!

Plate 101

Plate 102

Plate 101
    Cream Soup Bowl with Liner. Don't expect to find these in the colored glazes — they're technically Century, but collectors enjoy adding them to their Riviera. Demitasse cups and saucers, egg cups, and 8" plates may also be found, but only in ivory. A cream soup in ivory with gold bands has been reported.

Plate 102
    Tidbit Tray, 4½" Jug, Utility Bowl, Salt and Pepper Shakers. Here are more Century items. You will find the shakers in Riviera colors, and the two-tier tidbit tray has been reported in mauve blue as well. But the jug (a size between the batter pitcher and the syrup) and the utility bowl were never part of the Riviera line. One collector reports the earliest backstamp she has in her Century collection indicates a 1933 production date.

Plate 103

Plate 104
    Bowls: Baker, Nappy, Fruit, Oatmeal. Left to right: Baker, oval with straight sides, 9" long; Nappy, 7¼" diameter; Baker, oval with curved sides 9" long. In front: Fruit, 5½"; Oatmeal, 6". The oatmeal is sightly deeper than the fruit bowl and is rather scarce.

Plate 105
    Butter Dishes, Creamer and Sugar Bowl, Covered Jug. The covered jug, shown here in green, is really quite hard to find. The larger ½-lb. butter dish is more readily found than the smaller and is available in mauve blue, rose, spruce green, light green, turquoise, maroon, cobalt blue, red, ivory, and in both Fiesta and Harlequin yellow. The ¼-lb. size is rare in turquoise and cobalt. In Plate 103 you'll see an example in mauve blue that still has the original Riviera sticker. For further information on the butter dish, see Plate 159.

Plate 104

Plate 105

Plate 106

Sauce Boat. These are easy to find and are very similar to the creamer — just a bit longer.

Plate 107

Batter Set. Complete with tray in cobalt, covered syrup pitcher in red, and tall covered jug in green (used for mixing, storing, and pouring pancake and waffle batter), these sets are quite unique since they utilize one of the rare cobalt blue pieces and the cover for the tall jug. This is the standard color combination for these sets. Until we received the photo in Plate 109, the jug complete with the lid had been reported in only green and ivory. Here you see a very unusual batter set and a very attractive one, entirely in red. Occasionally you may find a set in ivory either with floral or scrollwork decals similar to those shown in Plates 108 and 110, but these are rare.

Plate 111

Casserole. A very nice piece and one that may prove difficult to find, the large size of these casseroles along with their distinctive styling and wonderful colors make them spectacular additions to your Riviera collections.

Plate 106

Plate 107

Plate 108

Plate 109

Plate 110

Plate 111

Plate 112

Plate 112
    Teapot, Teacups and Saucers. The collectors we questioned in our price survey tell us that the teapots are becoming scarce.

Plate 113
    Juice Pitcher, Juice Tumblers. The pitcher is scarce in any color but is standard in yellow. It's very rare in mauve blue, shown here. In the original sets, the tumblers were turquoise, mauve blue, red, yellow, light green, and ivory.

Plate 114
    Salt and Pepper Shakers, Syrup Pitcher, Deep Plate, Handled Tumblers. As you can see, there are six orange-like segments that make up the design of the salt and pepper shakers. These were borrowed from the Tango line; so you may find them in Tango's colors, too. Two pairs have been found in a true primary red glaze — origin unconfirmed. The covered syrup pitcher is a darling piece and rather hard to find. Ivory tumblers are scarce and often command high prices. Though not a Homer Laughlin product, you may find sets of glass tumblers (one style with a smooth surface, another with vertically paneled sides) each with a solid band of one of the Riviera colors at the rim. One set bought at auction was still in the original box marked 'Juanita Beverage Set, Rosenthal and Ruben, Inc. Binghampton, NY, 1938.' There were two each of the four colors (light green, mauve blue, yellow, and red) in four sizes: 3", 3½", 4", and 5¼". Matching swizzle sticks completed the forty-piece set.

Plate 113

Plate 114

Plate 115

   Compartment Plate. This in a new discovery, one we heard of just before we went to press. It measures 9¾". It was bought by a collector's friend who thought 'this looks like that stuff you collect.'

Plate 116

   Plates, 10", 9", 7", 6". The 10" plates are very hard to find. The 7" plate is sometimes found in cobalt blue, and collectors also report this size in Fiesta yellow. Perhaps, as one reader suggested, they were dipped in these colors to go with a Riviera/Fiesta ensemble such as in the ad in the chapter on advertising ephemera.

Plate 117

   Platters. Shown: 11½", no handles; 11¼", with closed handles. You'll also find 13¼" and 12" platters with the closed handles; and just as we were about to go to press an ivory example measuring 15⅞" was reported.

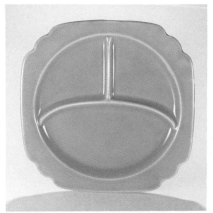

Plate 115

Plate 116

Plate 117

AMBERSTONE

This 'brown Fiesta' seems to have generated lots of enthusiasm among collectors; and it's easy to see why — especially when some of the hollowware pieces are found with the familiar Fiesta cast-indented trademark!

Amberstone was introduced in 1967, three years before the Fiesta line was restyled; yet the illustration on an old order blank shows that the sugar and creamer, cup, teapot, soup/cereal, casserole, and coffee server were from the same molds that were later used for Fiesta Ironstone. Only on the pieces that had relatively flat areas large enough to permit decoration do you find the black, machine-stamped underglaze pattern. The remainder were simply solid brown.

Sold under the trade name of Genuine Sheffield dinnerware, it was produced by HLC exclusively for supermarket promotions; and several large grocery store chains featured Amberstone as a premium. (For a listing of items offered, see 'Suggested Values' in back of book.)

Plate 118

Below are additional Amberstone shapes. The marmalade is shown in Plate 122, the mustard in Plate 119. Note the Ironstone casserole, flared fruit bowl, and sauce boat stand. Even though there was no butter dish listed in the Ironstone assortment (nor in the older Fiesta line), here's one in Amberstone, and there was one in the Casualstone line as well. (Photography in Plate 119 © Adam Anik)

Plate 119

Plate 120

Plate 121

Plate 122

CARNIVAL

Carnival was made exclusively for the Quaker Oats Company who gave it away to their customers, one piece packed in each box of Mother's Carnival Oats. While no records exist to verify the year in which it was first produced, we must assume it was in the late thirties or early forties by reason of the color assortment. Harlequin yellow, turquoise (both of which were first used by HLC in 1938), light green, and Fiesta red were evidently the original colors. The only mention of Carnival in company files was dated 1952; it lists these glazes: dark green, turquoise, gray, and Harlequin yellow. You'll also occasionally find examples in cobalt and ivory — notice the cups on the front of the box shown below. (The 1952 record also itemized the pieces in production at that time; these are listed with suggested values in the back of the book.) A company representative recalled that coupons were included in the boxes, redeemable for the larger pieces. What these might have been or when they were made, we have no way of knowing. Perhaps there were plates, bowls, and platters — if so, they may one day turn up to answer our questions.

Plate 123

Plate 124

CASUALSTONE

In 1970 Homer Laughlin produced a second line of dinnerware to be sold exclusively through supermarket promotions. This dinnerware was called Casualstone and was presented under the trade name 'Coventry.' The Antique Gold of the Fiesta Ironstone was decorated with an intricate gold machine-stamped design; which, like Amberstone, appeared on only the shallow items. An old order blank shows that it was less expensive than the Amberstone of three years previous, possibly because a color already in production was used. (For a listing of available items, see 'Suggested Values' in back of book.)

Plate 125

EPICURE

Epicure is a fifties line — with the fifties streamline styling and pastel colors. Anyone who remembers what a great era that was for growing up can tell you about pink and gray. Argyle socks were pink and gray! If your sweater was pink, your skirt or corduroys were gray. Turquoise was popular in home decorating — even down to appliances. And these were the colors of Epicure: Dawn Pink, Charcoal Gray, Turquoise Blue, and Snow White.

The designer was Don Schreckengost, who also designed Rhythm. We can find no information pinpointing production dates, but collectors tell us that virtually all of their Epicure is stamped 1955. The only exception ever reported was a set of plates in pink that were marked 1960. The line consisted of the following items:

Bowls:	Cereal/Soup	Casseroles: Covered Vegetable, Individual
	Fruit	Coffeepot, 10"
	Nappy, 8"	Creamer
	Nappy, 9"	Gravy Bowl
Platter, Large Oval		Ladle, 5½"
Salt and Pepper Shakers		Nut Dish
Sugar Bowl with Lid		Pickle (Small Oval Platter)
Teacup and Saucer		Plates: Dessert, 6½"
2-Tier Tidbit Tray		Snack, 8½"
		Dinner, 10"

The nut dish could pass for a butter pat; and one collector tells us that of the eleven in his collection, all are turquoise.

Plate 126

Plate 126

Tidbit, Creamer, Cereal/Soup, Sugar Bowl, Salt Shaker, Cup and Saucer, Individual Casserole. Very nearly the same size as the sugar bowl, the individual casserole (shown in Charcoal Gray) is very hard to find.

Epicure is not easy to find but represents an exciting challenge to many collectors. Dealers tell us that it sells well due to its famous-name designer and the present strong interest in the designs and colors of the fifties.

Plate 127

Coffeepot, Plates, Nappy, Gravy Bowl, Ladle, Covered Vegetable Casserole. The pink nappy is 9" (8¾"); plates are 10" and 6½". The turquoise gravy bowl holds a black ladle.

Plate 127

Plate 128

JUBILEE

Jubilee was presented by Homer Laughlin in 1948 in celebration of their 75th year of ceramic leadership. Shapes were simple and contemporary. It was offered in four colors: Celadon Green (blue-gray), Shell Pink, Mist Gray (lighter than Fiesta gray), and Cream Beige. The pastel juice set utilizing Fiesta molds is reported by collectors of this line to match the Jubilee glazes rather than those of Serenade (as we once thought). Kitchen Kraft bowls have been found in pink, blue-gray, and gray. Some are marked; others are not. Both the juice set and the bowls are shown. The juice set in Plate 128 was found in the original carton; its owners tell us that the floral decoration is hand painted and overglazed. It's the only decorated set we know of.

Jubilee shapes were also used as the basis for other lines. Skytone is a very attractive example, made in pastel blue with white handles and lid finials.

Plate 129

Plate 130

Plate 131

85

PASTEL NAUTILUS

HLC's Nautilus was made from the thirties into the fifties. It was often decaled; it was fancy-trimmed without decals; it was combined with Fiesta's first four colors to make the four 'Harmony' sets; and in 1940 (no other date marks have been reported) it was dipped in the pastel glazes of Serenade — pink, yellow, green, and blue — and offered to the public as Pastel Nautilus.

The line is scarce, to be sure, but very attractive; and, if you have the patience to work at it, a complete set would represent quite an accomplishment.

Shown in Plate 132 are 9", 7", and 6" plates; a teacup; a double egg cup; and a creamer. The casserole is in Plate 133 and the bowls in Plate 134 are as follows (clockwise): tab-handled soup, 6" cereal, 5" fruit, and cream soup. For a complete listing of available items, see 'Suggested Values' in the back of the book. (Photos by Shel Izen)

Plate 132

Plate 133

Plate 134

RHYTHM

With Rhythm steadily emerging from its 'sleeper' state, more accurate information than we had in the beginning is being pieced together by its dedicated fans. Those with large collections report back-stamps with dates indicating a span of production from 1950 to 1960. It was made in Harlequin yellow, chartreuse, gray, forest green, and burgundy (collectors call it maroon).

Rhythm shapes are simple and streamlined with a 'designer' look. Don Schreckengost was that designer, who early in 1982 was interviewed by a newsletter which was at that time being published in the East. In that interview, Mr. Schreckengost revealed that the spoon rest which we thought to be Harlequin was, in fact, a piece he had originated for the Rhythm line.

Several lines featuring decals on a white glaze were manufactured during the fifties utilizing Rhythm shapes. You will find several examples of these in the color plates. The spoon rests are often found with decals — Rhythm Rose and American Provincial are the most common. (For a complete listing of available items, see 'Suggested Values' in the back of the book.)

Plate 135

Plate 135
Casserole, Nappy, Soup, Fruit, Footed Cereal/Chowder. The 5½" fruit is shown center front; to the right is the 5½" footed cereal. The nappy (forest green) measures 9"; the soup is 8¼". The casserole is very hard to find.

Plate 136

Plate 136
   Plate, Sauce Boat, Soup/Cereal. The 8" yellow plate and the brown soup/cereal are marked Rhythm, though both are non-standard colors. The cobalt sauce boat (also found in black) and the black soup/cereal are unmarked and may have been made to go with another line, Cavalier. Does anyone have any information to offer concerning this line?

Plate 137
   Plates, Sauce Boat and Stand, Sugar Bowl, Snack Plate, Salt and Pepper Shakers. Plates measure 10", 9", 7", and 6"; the 7" and 8" (shown in Plate 136) are scarce. Though once considered non-existent, we have had reports of a few divided plates in maroon.

Plate 138
   Three-Tier Tidbit, Platters, Cup and Saucer, Teapot. These platters measure 13½" and 11½" long.

Plate 137

Plate 138

Plate 139

Plate 140

Plate 141

Plate 139
   Spoon Rest. These have been reported in yellow, turquoise, and forest green, and just recently we heard of one in medium green as well. An example in turquoise was found with a Harlequin label, so obviously these were sold with that line as well. You'll also see them in white with a decal decoration, but these are much less valuable.

Plate 140
   Calendar Plate. The company issued a calendar plate for a number of years, using whatever blanks were available.

Plate 141
   Mixing Bowls. These are the Kitchen Kraft bowls; this particular combination of color identifies them as Rhythm. They measure 10", 8", and 6"; and they have a dry foot. The gray bowls we used to list with Kitchen Kraft were more than likely part of this set, and my sources tell me that they've never seen gray in any but the 10" size. If you have any other information, let us hear from you.

Serenade

Serenade was a pastel dinnerware line that was produced for only three or four years from about 1939 (it was mentioned in the American Potter's brochure from the World's Fair) until the early forties. It was offered in four lovely pastel shades — yellow, green, pink, and blue. Although not well accepted by the public when it was introduced, today's collectors find its soft delicate hues and dainty contours appealing. There is growing interest in this elusive pattern, but prices are still relatively moderate.

Lug soups and teapots are rare; so are 10" plates. You may also find deep plates, 7" plates, 6" fruits, and 9" nappies to be scarce. Sugar bowls are harder to find than creamers, and the lid for the casserole (the only Kitchen Kraft piece dipped in Serenade colors) is virtually impossible to find — only two have ever been reported. (All photos with the exception of the KK casserole by Shel Izen.)

Plate 142

Plate 142
Chop Plate, 13"; Teapot; Creamer and Sugar Bowl; Cup and Saucer.

Plate 143

Plate 144

Plate 143
    Casserole. This is the standard Serenade casserole.

Plate 144
    Casserole, Kitchen Kraft. For many years, the lid to this casserole could not be found. Finally, only two or three years ago, two were reported, one in yellow and one in blue. For this update, a collector tells us of one he has found in ivory.

Plate 145
    Deep Plate; Nappy, 9"; Sauce Boat; Fruit Bowl, 6"; Lug (Tab-Handled) Soup Bowl.

Plate 146
    Plates, 10", 9", 6"; Platter, 12½"; Pickle Dish; Salt and Pepper Shakers.

Plate 145

Plate 146

TANGO

Tango was introduced in the late 1930s, made for promotion through Newberry's and the McLellan Stores Company, N.Y. City. For some reason, it was not a good seller — perhaps its rather Colonial design seemed a bit incongruous alongside other styles of colored dinnerware. Standard colors were spruce green, mauve blue, yellow, and maroon; but, as you can see in the color plate, a few pieces may also be found in Fiesta red.

The line was rather limited; all available items are shown below, although unconfirmed rumors occasionally circulate concerning the existence of an egg cup. Until the egg cup can be verified, we assume that the line consisted of a fruit bowl; deep plate; oval vegetable bowl; round nappy; casserole with lid; creamer and sugar bowl; cup and saucer; plates, 10", 9", 7", and 6"; platter; and salt and pepper shakers. The shakers should look very familiar to Riviera collectors. They were original with this line; but, since their shape was compatible, they were borrowed for use with Riviera.

Proving once again that value is a relative thing, our price survey (which represents a cross-section) indicated prices for Tango hadn't elevated to any great extent; but dyed-in-the-wool, dedicated Tango collectors tell us that to them their collections are worth much more than suggested 'book' prices because it is so scarce. And, we are sure, this is the sentiment of collectors of other minor lines as well.

The W. S. George Company made a line very similar to Tango, but their glazes are rather dull and the definition of the 'petals' somewhat indistinct in comparison. You'll be able to recognize Tango by the raised line just inside the shaped rim. (Photography © Adam Anik.)

Plate 147

WELLS ART GLAZE

If you like a real challenge, here's one for you! This line was produced from 1930 until at least 1935 in the colors shown — rust, peach, green, yellow — and a burnt orange matt similar to Fiesta red. It's a lovely design, and records list an extensive assortment. But because of its limited availability on today's market, values are still low. (For a complete listing of available items, see 'Suggested Values' in the back of the book.)

Plate 148

Plate 149

Plate 148
   Teapots. The teapot on the left is very scarce; very few have been reported. The shape is from a standard Homer Laughlin line called 'Empress.' On the right is the traditional Wells Art Glaze teapot; you'll see it again in Plate 152.

Plate 149
   Demitasse Pot, Individual Sugar and Creamer. Note the differences in the handles on the sugar bowl shown here and the one in Plate 152.

Plate 150

Plate 151

Plate 152

Plate 150
   Chop Plate, Covered Jug, Baker, Sugar Bowl with Lid, Teacup and Saucer, Demitasse Cup and Saucer, Handled Coffee Cup. The handled chop plate measures 10", the covered jug is 9", and the oval baker is 9" long. The cup on the far right is inscribed 'Coffee' and is 4¾" tall.

Plate 151
   Batter Set. The covered jug, covered syrup pitcher, and oval tray comprise this very rare set. You may also find these in white with floral decals.

Plate 152
   Plates, Teapot, Teacup and Saucer, Creamer and Sugar Bowl. Shown are the 9", 8", and 6" plates, and a square one that measures 8".

ORANGE TREE BOWLS

Though we've always referred to these as the 'orange tree' bowls because of their resemblance to Fenton's carnival glass pattern of the same name, some collectors call them 'peach tree.' Whatever you choose to call them, they're very scarce — especially the small bowl. We suspect these were designed by Rhead due to the stylized tree motif very similar to designs he used earlier in his career. They range in size from 5" up to 10", and though they're more common in turquoise, they've also been found in ivory, yellow, and pumpkin. On rare occasions, the ivory is decorated with stripes. One collector has a bowl with a red stripe on the top of the rim, another tells us that his has three green stripes — one inside the rim, one outside the rim, and one on top.

Plate 153

FIVE-PETAL DAISY

Here's another line for those of you who enjoy a challenge. The name isn't official, merely descriptive. The official company name for this shape is 'Marigold,' and it was used as a basis for several decaled lines. This pieces is backstamped 1937, so it was made early in the days of HLC's campaign to promote this type of colored dinnerware. This is the deep plate in the company's standard light green glaze.

Plate 154

CONCHITA

When first introduced in the late thirties, Homer Laughlin's Mexican-style dinnerware lines were met with great enthusiasm. Speaking of Mexicana, which would prove to be one of their bestsellers, a trade paper from May, 1938 had this to say:

> When this Homer Laughlin pattern was first exhibited last July at the House Furnishing Show, it was an immediate smash hit. Its popularity has grown steadily ever since, and retailers have found it a constant and dependable source of profit. It started the vogue for the Mexican motif in crockery decoration which has since swept the country.

> And small wonder! For this Mexicana pattern is smart, colorful, and attractive. It embodies the old-world atmosphere of Mexico with the modern verve and personality which is so appealing to American housewives. Applied to the pleasing, beautifully designed Homer Laughlin shapes, it presents a bestseller of the first order.

Conchita is a line that utilizes Century shapes. A fairly extensive line of Kitchen Kraft was offered as well, though collectors tell us that this line is not as plentiful as Kitchen Kraft with the Mexican decal. Virtually all Conchita is trimmed in red. If you have any with blue trim, please let us know.

The popularity of these Mexican-style lines seems to be somewhat regional, according to our price survey, with collectors from the west coast tending to value them most highly. This makes it very difficult to offer accurate, across-the-board book prices. To avid collectors of this type of dinnerware, their collections are worth much more than 'book.'

Plate 155

Plate 156

Plate 157

Plate 155

Oven–Serve Casserole, Oven-Serve Underplate, Cake Plate, Covered Jar, and Covered Jug. The casserole is marked Handy Andy on the base; and, although it's hard to see in the photo, there is an embossed design at the rim of the lid as well as around the outside of the underplate above it. These two pieces were found together, complete with the metal base — a rare find. You'll find this casserole with other decals, one a wheat and flower motif.

Plate 156

Platter, 11½"; Creamer and Sugar Bowl; Cup and Saucer. The tumblers were featured in the Fiesta Ensembles (See Plate 217); they look especially good with the Mexican lines. There were two sets — one comprised of the three directly in front of the platter. A second consisted of the one to the far left, a larger tumbler with the Fiesta dancing girl, and a small juice glass with a guitar. These fired-on designs can be found on both plain and lightly paneled glasses. A third set along with a matching pitcher is shown in the chapter called 'Go-Alongs.'

Plate 157

Kitchen Kraft Server, Underplate, Individual Casserole. Notice the original label on the underplate; this is a decaled version of the mysterious underplate that was mentioned in the chapter on Fiesta Kitchen Kraft. None has ever been found in the solid colors.

Plate 158

Plate 158
   Kitchen Kraft Jars, Small, Medium, and Large; and Salt and Pepper Shakers. These are turned to show the decals on both sides.

HACIENDA

This is a rather extensive line and is probably second only to Mexicana in availability. Both patterns are on Century shapes with few exceptions. Unlike Mexicana, however, you'll find no matching Kitchen Kraft line. However, at least one large Kitchen Kraft mixing bowl has been found, apparently a special order by a Birmingham, Alabama, furniture store.

Plate 159

Plate 160

Plate 159

Butter Dish, ½-Lb.; Teapot; Cream Soup Bowl. All of these items are relatively hard to find. Because of the consistency with which these butter dishes have been used in Century-based Mexican lines, we assumed them to be Century; but one of the photographs sent to us to use in this edition proved us wrong (again). The butter bottom even looks like Century because of its striped tab-like extensions; but, if you'll look at the La Hacienda pattern on the Jade shape shown in Plate 280, you'll see that to be correct we should be calling these butter dishes Jade, not Century. The Hacienda teapot turns up more often than its matching casserole. The reverse is true of Century Mexicana, and only the casserole has been reported in Century Conchita.

Plate 160

Plate, 10"; Fruit Bowl, 5"; Cup and Saucer; and Sugar Bowl.

Plate 161

Plate 162

Plate 163

Plate 161

   Dinner Bell, Butter Dish. The bell has the Hacienda decal, but it's very doubtful that it was produced by HLC. The round butter dish is hard to find; this one we guarantee to be Century.

Plate 162

   Covered Jug. Because this piece is complete with the lid, it's twice as nice. This is a rare item.

Plate 163

   Casserole. This piece is large and very attractive, but not at all easy to find.

Plate 164

Plate 165

Plate 164
  Nautilus Deep Plate; Platter, 13"; Plate 9"; Casserole; Creamer and Sugar Bowl; Sauce Boat; Teacup and Saucer. Hacienda on the Nautilus shape is rare, and the line is doubly unusual in that the color is white not ivory.

Plate 165
  Swing Creamer and Sugar Bowl; Utility Tray; Casserole with Lid; Luncheon and Bread and Butter Plates; Fruit Bowl; Cup and Saucer; Platter, 11½"; Covered Sauce Boat with Saucer; and Salt and Pepper Shakers. This is another rare example of the Hacienda decal applied to one of Homer Laughlin's standard dinnerware shapes other than Century; and again, the background color is white. Mexicana and Conchita also appear on Swing (not shown). (Photography © Adam Anik)

MAX-I-CANA

   We've never found an official name for this pattern anywhere in the company's files, but it's been dubbed Max-i-cana by collectors. The siesta-taking Mexican snoozing under his sombrero amid jugs, jars, and cacti decorates the shape known as 'Yellowstone' in Plate 167 and looks just as much at home on ivory Fiesta in Plate 166.

Plate 166

Plate 167

Plate 166
   Max-i-cana Fiesta Platter, Cup and Saucer, Fruit. The fruit is the smaller 4¾" size.

Plate 167
   Max-i-cana Yellowstone Platter, Sauce Boat Liner, Sauce Boat, Egg Cup, Rolled-edge Egg Cup, Casserole, ½-Lb. Butter Dish, Creamer and Sugar Bowl. The platter measures 13½"; directly in front of it, the sauce boat liner is 8½". The teapot has never been found.

MEXICALI

Plate 168

Plate 169

Plate 170

Plates 168 and 170

Until this edition, Virginia Rose was the only shape we knew of to be decorated with the Mexicali decal. Plates 168 and 170 show a set of yellow Harlequin Mexicali. This must have been a very exciting acquisition. Not a single other piece has ever surfaced that we know of, but the owner was lucky enough to buy the set intact.

Plate 169

Swing is the shape shown here with the 11" platter decorated in the Mexicali pattern; the creamer and sugar bowl are in the Conchita design. Both are marked 'Eggshell,' a term used to indicate HLC's lightweight semi-porcelain.

Plate 171

Plate 171
Virginia Rose, shown here with the Mexicali decal. Here you see the small serving bowl, the 8½" platter, and the 8" plate. You'll have to look long and hard for this and both of the two previous shapes you've seen in the Mexicali line.

Plate 172
Three rare pieces in Century Mexicana: teapot, after dinner cup and saucer (nine are known), and deep rimless bowl. (Photography © Adam Anik)

Plate 173
Platter, 15"; Vegetable Bowl, 9"; Lug Soup Bowl; Creamer and Sugar Bowl.

MEXICANA

Mexicana is the most readily-available of all the Mexican-style lines produced by Homer Laughlin. It was introduced in 1937; and, like the others, the company selected Century shapes as the basis for this line as well. You'll sometimes find pieces marked 'Mexicana' with a gold backstamp. Although occasionally found with yellow, green, and blue bands, red is by far the most plentiful. We've had a single report of some pieces with brown trim as well as some with no trim at all. (Photography in Plate 172 © Adam Anik)

Several other companies produced similarly decorated lines with a decided Mexican flavor — Paden City, Vernon Kilns, Crown, and Stetson, to name but a few. Besides the Mexican lines shown in the color plates, HLC also made Arizona, decorated with a large green cactus, adobe house, yucca plant, and pottery jug; however, this line is seldom seen.

Plate 172

Plate 173

107

Plate 174

Plate 175

Plate 176

Plate 174
  Jug (Open), Teapot.

Plate 175
  Casserole with Lid.

Plate 176
  Kitchen Kraft Cake Plate, Covered Jug, Stacking Refrigerator Set, Salt and Pepper Shakers.

Plate 177

Plate 178

Plate 177

Virginia Rose — this time as a very rare variation of the Mexicana line. Shown are the 9½" and 6" plates, teacup and saucer, and the 5" fruit bowl.

Plate 178

Nautilus 'Eggshell' pieces shown here are all dated 1937. Note the blue-line trim and the stark white background. This line is very, very rare. Shown are the 13" platter, 9" and 7" plates, 5" fruit, creamer and sugar bowl, and the teacup and saucer.

RANCHERA

Plate 179

Plate 179

    This final south-of-the-border dinnerware line utilizes the Nautilus shape again, this time with a decal we've never seen before nor do we have any knowledge of it's official name. But the collector who is sharing this find with us suggests we call it 'Ranchera.' Here can be seen the 9", 7", and 6" plates; the 11" platter; an oval vegetable bowl; the 6" oatmeal; the 5" fruit; and the teacup and saucer.

GO-ALONGS

'Go-alongs' is a term that has been coined by collectors to refer to metal parts (frames, handles, etc.) woodenware, flatware, and a variety of other products whose style and colors were obviously made to accessorize the colored dinnerware lines that were made by HLC as well as many other companies. This aspect of collecting is very popular with many. Others feel that because it's in 'the book,' it is often tagged 'Fiesta,' and sold as such when, of course, it is not. We must remember that Homer Laughlin was in the business to make dinnerware — not appliances, metal bowls, or any of the other items you will see in this section. The Fiesta patent was issued for the manufacture of nothing but dinnerware; so no matter what else you may encounter that carries the name 'Fiesta,' please don't be fooled into believing it to be genuine. For instance, you'll see a Fiesta Quikut flatware set in Plate 208. It would look great with your genuine Fiesta, but Fiesta it's not. And a reader has sent in a photo of her 'Fiesta' tablecloth. Though the logo is very similar, the style of the lettering is entirely different and the dancing girl is facing you. Also, beware — we have known of schemes meant to mislead collectors by using fake Fiesta ink stamps on items HLC never even dreamed of making.

Accessories shown in Plates 180 and 181 are decidedly Mexican in flavor and their bright primary colors would be great with any of Homer Laughlin's solid-color dinnerware lines in the more vivid tones. The water set is decorated on one side with a dancing senorita and on the other with a guitar-strumming Mexican fellow. You'll find the tumblers in three sizes: 4¾" (8-oz.), 3¾" (8-oz.), and 3¾" (4-oz.) The pitcher holds 64 ounces and is 9½" tall. Wooden napkin rings and placecard holders, cord-wrapped enameled tumblers, and coasters in a wireware frame could certainly create a party atmosphere when mixed, for instance, with a setting of Riviera.

Plate 180

Plate 181

While we once thought the metal fitting for the cream soup bowl, the marmalade, and the cake plate (in Plate 182) were most certainly marketed by an outside company, we now have a Xerox copy of a company order sheet that shows not only these but the #610 salad service set pictured in Plate 183. The Xerox also shows the three items in the line drawings below: the condiment set — mustard, salt and pepper shakers; the '#608 8" casserole' (this is our new promotional casserole, see Fiesta color plates); and '#609 double tidbit with folding stand.' Since we first pictured these drawings, several of the casserole frames have turned up, but as far as we know, the one on the right has yet to be found. These items comprise their '#600 Gift Assortment of Colored Ware'; and, because the colors listed are red, green, blue, and yellow, we assume that these were offered in the early days of production. There is another frame that will hold both the marmalade and the mustard; it's not shown in this edition. And you may find a metal rotating base that turns the six-part Fiesta relish tray into a Lazy Susan server.

The three-tier tidbit tray in Plate 184 bears need for a little discussion. Obviously if the metal fittings were available, either old or newly made, anyone could create this item. This one has the ring handle which some collectors feel is the 'correct' handle, but you'll also find some with the triangular finial such as you can see on the Amberstone tray in our color plates — it's also shown in the company's Amberstone advertising material in our files. We questioned a long-time dealer who agrees that when buying this piece, you should inspect it carefully; these were being made with new fittings by an individual only a few years ago.

Harlequin and Riviera have had their fair share of metal enhancements as well. Plates 185 through 189 attest to that. The tumbler is fitted with a chrome soda fountain-style base and handle, the donkey is laden with salt and pepper shaker saddle bags, and we call the Harlequin 36s bowl a nut dish — it was made by some enterprising company simply by adding a little chrome and a glass knob. The Riviera items are newly reported — note the hardware on the last three examples, identical down to the glass ball finials. They're all obviously the work of the same company. The two-tier tidbit is usually found only in ivory, but one has been found in green complete with a green glass knob. Whether or not at some time these were marketed by HLC is anybody's guess at this point. Evidently there were promotions offered by the company for which there is no documentation, so who is to say.

In the early 1940s, the Hankscraft Company marketed their electric egg cooker in service sets that included the cooker as shown in Plate 190, 'four vari-colored Fiesta egg cups (red, yellow, blue, and green), ivory (pottery) poaching dish, Fiesta salt and pepper shakers, and maple plywood tray.' They called this set the 'Fiesta Egg Service' and sold it for $9.50 to $13.70, depending upon whose catalog you happened to be using. The set as shown has not been listed in any of these catalogs but is the one more often found. Obviously, these egg cups are not Fiesta. They're made of the same material as the cooker itself (identical to the one pictured with the Fiesta set mentioned above) and are smaller than genuine Fiesta egg cups. Remember, this was a Hankscraft product — not made by Homer Laughlin, not genuine Fiesta.

A similar idea featured a Westinghouse sandwich grill on a tray large enough to accomodate it, a small cutting board, and several pieces of Fiesta: the utility tray with what appears in the photograph to be the center of the relish tray nestled in one end (!), a stack of small plates, salt and pepper shakers, a mustard, and a marmalade.

Marketed during the forties (as far as we know, not by HLC), the 'Fiesta' popcorn set in Plate 191 is enameled tinware; note the familiar Fiesta-type rings and colors. The tidbit in Plate 193 features the same type of metal bowls in a cloverleaf wireware stand.

In Plates 192 and 198, you'll see two styles of beverage carriers — one wrought iron, the other wireware. As far as we know, these were not marketed by HLC; but since we now know the company actually sold more of these accessories than we once thought they did, we hesitate to be entirely confident about it. Watch for new reproductions of the carrier in Plate 192.

Rattan-wrapped handles have been found to accessorize several items. In Plate 194 one has been fitted to a mixing bowl, creating an ice bucket. It's an exact match to the metal handle offered in combination with the chop plate in the 1939–'43 selling campaign. These have been found in sizes to fit the 7", 9", and 10" plates (which also fits the relish tray) as well as both sizes of the chop plates. We'd almost bet these were routed through HLC.

Plate 182

Plate 183

Plate 184

Wooden go-alongs are popular with collectors. The 20" Lazy Susan in Plate 198 is a Fiestawood piece by the G. H. Specialty Co., Milwaukee, Wisconsin. Its center insert is 'Intaglio,' made by Indiana Glass during the 1930s. It is a five-part 10" plate with intaglio seafood and vegetables that features a bunch of celery in the long center section. The very large party server in Plate 202 is also Fiestawood. The center section is for hors d'oeuvres; it's pierced to hold toothpicks, and it can be removed. Plates 196, 199, and 200 show more Fiestawood. The first two are salad bowls — note the brightly colored band of rings that is characteristic of all Fiestawood we have seen. The tray in Plate 200 is another for hors d'oeuvres; the fish in the center is pierced to hold toothpicks. The border decoration is especially effective — stripes in festive colors punctuated by decals of a snoozing Mexican. In Plate 195 is woodenware by an unidentified company; paired with the revolving metal base and a 15" Fiesta chop plate it becomes a Lazy Susan. We've also seen nappies in fruit-decorated wooden holders.

Also in Plate 198, the teapot is converted to a dripolator with the addition of the 5½" metal assembly. Reticulated metal holders with handles like the one above the teapot are shown on a second Xerox we have advertising the #109-12 Assortment package. It includes the 10" KK pie plate and platter, the 8½" and 9½" Fiesta nappies, and the promotional casserole we've pictured for the first time in this edition. These Xerox copies along with the fact that the promotional casserole shown in the color plates was found in an unopened carton convinced us that this casserole was really an HLC product, even though the company told us years ago that it was not.

Plate 185   **Plate 186**   **Plate 187**

Plate 188   **Plate 189**

114

Plate 190

Plate 191

Plate 192

Plate 193

Plate 194

Plate 195

Plate 196

Plate 197

Plate 198

We've heard of some strange things, but none have ever topped the kitchen cabinet shown in Plate 201. Note the red, green, turquoise, and yellow trim. Matching wood canisters and a brass plate inscribed 'Fiesta' complete this unlikely cupboard. We've seen photos of a similar cabinet, this one stamped on the back in ink: NO-U-68-F-Fiesta. These have a central cupboard that houses a flour sifter, tambour compartment, and utensil and bread drawers. Attached side cabinets are shelved inside.

Do-it-yourself decals (Plate 203) were readily available in 5-and-10¢ stores, and collectors have reported finding sheets of them such as the one shown here. The back of the sheet reads 'Designs by Betty Best, Festivalware, Set #5001.' They were produced in 1945 by the American Decalcomania Co. of Chicago and New York. You may find tiles that have been commercially decorated with these decals and shelf paper by Betty Brite that also features Fiesta dishes.

Just about as unlikely as a kitchen cabinet is the ash stand in Plate 204. The design of the metal stand is right out of the fifties and so is the Fiesta deep plate in chartreuse.

Plate 199

Plate 200

Plate 201

Plate 202

Tin kitchenware items such as those in Plates 205 through 207 were popular during the late thirties and forties. One company who made them was Owens-Illinois Can Co. They called their line 'Fiesta' (what else) and decorated it in 'Roman stripes in red, blue, and green on yellow.' The set consisted of canisters, a bread box, a dust pan, a garbage can, and a kitchen stool. As you can see, some of these tinware items were decaled with Fiesta-like dinnerware. A three-tiered vegetable bin and a wastebasket have been found to match. The breadbox in Plate 205 is decorated in pots and plants with a Mexican flavor. In our files we have a photo of a 12" turquoise chop plate to which has been added a tinware cake-safe top. The lid is enameled in a matching turquoise, and it's topped with a wooden knob.

Catalin (plastic)-handled stainless steel flatware by Sta-Brite was part of the 'Fiesta Ensembles' offered by the company in the early years of production (you'll see one in Plate 217). Note the name on the box of the smaller flatware set. This is the 'Fiesta' assortment we mentioned earlier. The large set in Plate 209 was assembled by a collector-friend of ours who also built the lovely chest that contains it. Many other patterns of Catalin-handled cutlery were made during this period, and several of them were teamed with colored dinnerware lines of other companies. Prices vary greatly — if you buy it a piece at a time, you should be able to buy at much lower prices proportionately than if you purchase a place setting, especially if salad forks or tablespoons are included. Boxed sets that contain service for eight or more with several extra serving pieces go at a premium.

Plate 203

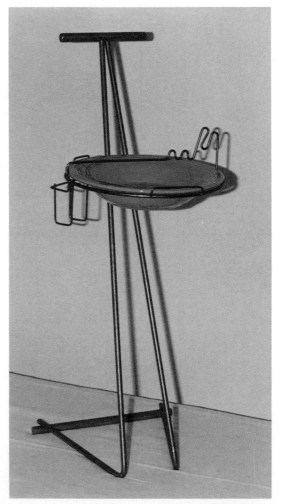

Plate 204

Plate 205

Plate 206

Plate 207

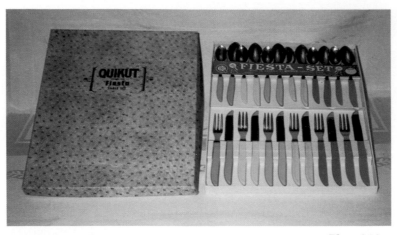

Plate 208

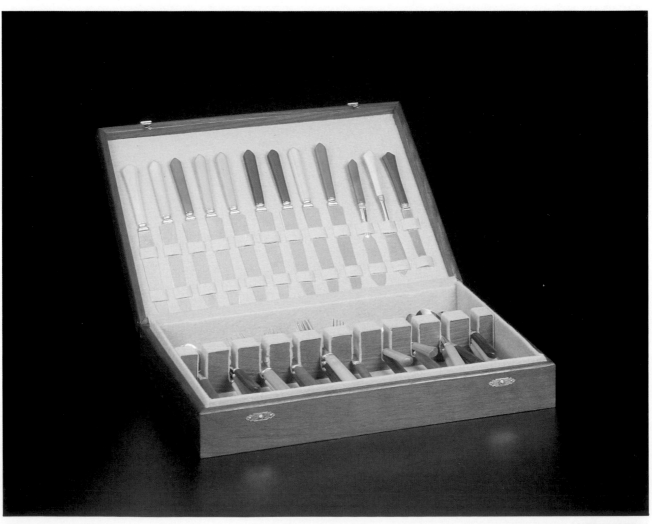

Plate 209

COMMERCIAL ADAPTATIONS
AND EPHEMERA

Advertising materials — especially HLC's own — make interesting and desirable additions to our collections and they are certainly worthwhile investments. The company's price lists contain a wealth of information. They've been our main source of study; and, as new ones are found to fill in the gaps, we may yet learn more about the various dinnerware lines. Fiesta price lists are much easier to find (only a few have been found on the other lines), but even they are scarce. Two of these are shown in Plate 210, and in Plates 211, 212, and 213 you'll see Riviera, Fiesta Kitchen Kraft, and Harlequin price lists.

The cardboard store display in Plate 214 captures and conveys the festive appeal of Fiesta dinnerware. This particular one never left the HLC pottery, but a few collectors report being lucky enough to have found one elsewhere. There were actually two of the small side sections; one is missing from this example. You can judge its size from the mixing bowls on either side. A collector sent us a photo of another display, this one of Spanish ladies dancing down a cobblestone piazza with a big villa in the background and a guitar player to the left — all recessed behind a large archway and a platform for the Fiesta.

Plate 210

Examples of original packaging material such as shown in Plates 215 and 216 are very popular with collectors — especially those with the dancing girl logo. Cartons in Plate 215 are for 5½" bowls (far right), saucers (center), cups (left) and 8½" nappy (rear); a service for four is contained in the box in Plate 216. These date from 1959 to 1969.

Plate 217 shows a full-color display ad that appeared in the Des Moines Register and Tribune on March 2, 1939. It advertises the company's 'Fiesta Ensemble' as described in an earlier chapter. Only four basic colors were offered along with matching Mexican glassware tumblers. A collector who owns a copy of this ad describes the ash tray/coasters shown above the table as 'clear glass — no design except a waffle pattern.' Note the interesting blend of Fiesta and Riviera.

The commercial uses of Fiesta pieces in advertising and television — even as props in Broadway shows — have become so commonplace that we can't list them all . . . cereal and toothpaste ads, in featured recipes; you've probably seen many. Or how about 'Fiesta Wear, ladies blouses dyed to match those dishes.' (No, we're not joking.) Plates 219 through 224 are examples of many of the ways our colored dinnerware lines have been used commercially. The punch-outs in Plate 218 were distributed by the National Dairy Council in 1959; there were eight in the series. In 1960 these were issued again; this time the series was expanded from eight to twelve. In Plate 219 is a soup can label that features the Harlequin cream soup bowl in a color that appears to be medium green. We didn't have room in this edition to show you some illustrations that were included in a 1937 electric stove promotional pamphlet, 'Meals Go Modern Electrically,' all of which feature kitchens and tables decked out with Fiesta dinnerware as well as some of its contemporaries. We recently received a greeting card with three luscious fuchsia tulips whose long stems curve forward from the lip of a yellow disk pitcher — even Hallmark designers appreciate those wonderful Art Deco lines.

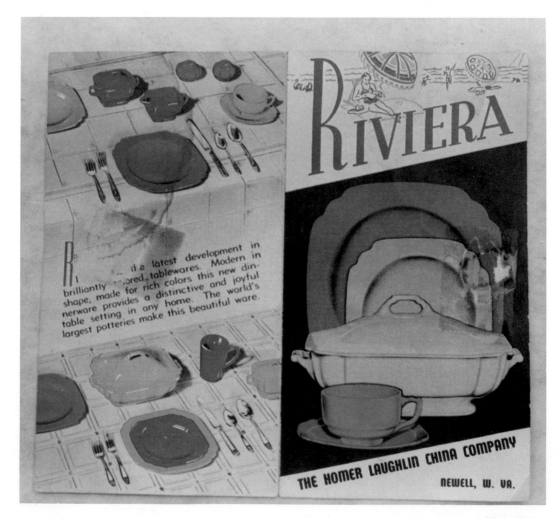

Plate 211

Guaranteed
fiesta
KITCHEN KRAFT
U.S.A.

JARS, COVERED
SMALL, MEDIUM, LARGE

JUG, COVERED
LARGE

MIXING BOWLS
10" — 8" — 6"

SPOON — FORK
CAKE SERVER

CASSEROLES, COVERED
8½" — 7½" — INDIVIDUAL

4 PC.
REFRIGERATOR
SET

PIE PLATE
CAKE PLATE

SALT AND PEPPER
PLATES — 6" — 9"

NOW...the parade of color invades the kitchen, too! In Fiesta Kitchen Kraft we offer you a ware that combines rich, colorful beauty with a high degree of practical utility. For baking, for table use, for refrigerator or kitchen cabinet storage, for every demand of the busy kitchen, Kitchen Kraft provides items eminently suitable. This line comes in four lovely colors . . . Green, Yellow, Blue and Red . . . all brilliant and eye-catching, making possible numerous attractive color combinations. Delightfully shaped, excellent in texture, material and design, Fiesta Kitchen Kraft is yet reasonable in price and may be conveniently bought by the piece.

Plate 212

HARLEQUIN

The new Harlequin Pottery offers a gift to table gaiety. It brings the magic of bright, exciting color to the table, dresses the festive board with pleasantness and personality, makes of every meal a cheerful and companionable occasion.

The new ware comes in four lovely colors . . . Yellow, Green, Red, and Blue . . . and offers the hostess endless possibilities for creating interesting and appealing color effects on her table. All the colors are brilliant and eye-catching . . . designed to go together effectively in any combination the hostess may desire. To set a table with Harlequin is an adventure in decoration. Plates are of one color, cups of another, saucers and platters of another . . . you can give free range to your artistic instincts.

And it is very easy to build up a comprehensive set of Harlequin in whatever items and colors you desire, because it may be bought by the piece at extremely reasonable prices.

Sold Exclusively by
F. W. WOOLWORTH CO. STORES

POTTERY

Plate 213

Plate 214

The syrup base in Plate 220 is still full of Duchess brand tea that was sold in it many years ago; the label and the cork stopper are completely intact.

For several years the Lazarus Company issued Fiesta items such as the yellow fruit bowl in Plate 221 to commemorate their anniversaries. This piece is for their 87th year; a plate was issued for their 88th, an egg cup for their 89th, and a tumbler for their 90th. Tom and Jerry mugs have also been reported.

The ash tray seems to have been a popular item for advertising use. In previous issues we've shown other examples; the one in Plate 222 carries not only the Fiesta ink stamp on the back but the name of the Sears, Roebuck Company as well.

If you enjoy collecting this type of memorabilia, try to find the October 10, 1936, issue of the *Saturday Evening Post*. Inside is a two-page Armstrong floor-covering ad with a vintage kitchen-dining room fairly blooming with Fiesta. Another ad featuring Fiesta appeared in Better Homes and Gardens, December 1936.

A few years ago, the Dard Mfg. Co. of Evanston, Illinois, produced an item that for awhile caused a bit of excitement in the Fiesta world. In a box marked 'Fiesta Coasters, Tag-Master Line ASI 4850' — exactly the right size to hold the relish tray center — they marketed a set of four plastic advertising coasters. Someone, perhaps less than honest or just misinformed, tried to perpetuate the 'Fiesta Coaster Hoax' by replacing the plastic coasters with the relish center.

Plate 215

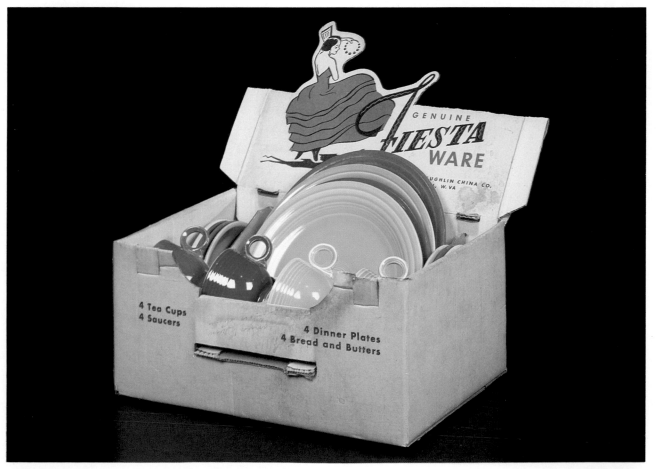

Plate 216

White, not ivory, is the color of the advertising mugs in Plate 227. Collectors have reported a variety of these — one decorated with a caricature of Lucille Ball signed 'Love, Lucy' from the Desilu Studios is especially unique. The Jackson Custom China Co. of Falls Creek, Pennsylvania, has made mugs very similar to the Tom and Jerry. We've heard of them in brown with a cream interior and (hold on to your hats) more recently in maroon. How'd you like a set of those for your morning coffee! The same company has also produced a child's set consisting of a divided plate, a 6" bowl, and the Tom and Jerry, all in white decorated with a blue stenciled Donald Duck and friends. Note the mug in Plate 225. This is the new-style mug; it was presented by the State of West Virginia to commemorate the introduction of the newly redesigned Fiesta Ware line.

T and Js in Fiesta colors with advertising are rare, though it isn't uncommon to find examples in white with color inside (and some will be found without the advertising). These were produced during the late sixties into the early seventies; interior colors are turquoise, yellow, rose, amberstone, or turf green.

Plate 217

Plate 218

Plate 219

Plate 220

Plate 221

Plate 222

Plate 223

Plate 224

In Plate 228 are a series of six mugs distributed at annual meetings of Buick Management and their Retirement Club members, 1964 through 1969. Represented on the mugs are a 1924 Model 48 Buick, a 1904 Model B Buick, a 1936 Buick Special, a 1941 Buick Roadmaster, a 1908 Model 10 Buick, and a 1916 Model D Buick. Plate 226 illustrates the coasters that accompanied them; these are hard to find. There is also an ash tray inscribed '1963 Buick Management Meeting, Dec. 11–12.' It is 8¾" in diameter, has six cigarette rests, and is raised in the center.

Plate 225

Plate 226

Plate 227

Plate 228

129

A WORD TO THE WISE

As any collector of colored dinnerware knows, there are many lines with characteristics very similar to Homer Laughlin's. Not just Fiesta but in fact nearly any of HLC's solid-color patterns has a look-alike. Potteries made a practice of reproducing each other's colors and designs, especially those that had been proven successful on the market. For instance, Bauer's Monterey (1934) is very similar to Fiesta both in color and in design. The cake stand shown in plate 231 is a good example of that line. The band of rings, weight, and feel of this piece might cause even a seasoned collector to have second thoughts. In addition to the turquoise shown here, Monterey also came in maroon, yellow, green, orange-red, medium blue, and ivory. Bauer's earlier line called Ring (1932), though with chunkier, heavier lines, was also produced in the bright solid glazes.

Plate 229 contains a wonderful array of shapes and colors. These teapots represent lines that were Fiesta's contemporaries; they were produced by various manufacturers, all located in Ohio. The green pot is Taylor, Smith & Taylor's Vistosa, a line styled with pastry-crimped rims and handles daintily trimmed with tiny blossoms. Vistosa was made in Fiesta-like red, cobalt blue, yellow, and light green. Caliente (the cobalt teapot) was made by Paden City; its streamlined styling featured hollowware whose bases were designed with four petal-like feet; it's colors were identical to Vistosa's. The large red teapot (top right) is Valencia by Shawnee, and the smaller pot (bottom right) is part of Knowles' Yorktown line. (Photography © Adam Anik)

Serenade's counterpart was Lu-Ray by Taylor, Smith & Taylor. Pastel colors and simple lines were characteristic of both. Rhythm had a twin in Universal's Ballerina line. W. S. George made Rainbow, which is very easily confused with HLC's Tango line. And many other companies, among them Vernon Kilns, Franciscan, Metlox, Coors, and French Saxon China, produced solid-color dinnerware as well.

Plate 229

Even the Mexican decaled lines had competition. Stetson made Mexicalis, Paden City had Patio, Mt. Clemons produced Old Mexico, and Tia Juana was a line of the Knowles Company. So it is obvious that it takes a certain amount of study and caution to become a knowledgeable collector. To become familiar with the lines mentioned above, we recommend *The Collector's Encyclopedia of American Dinnerware* by Jo Cunningham. If you are a beginning collector intending to limit your buying to a particular line of Homer Laughlin's, use this book as your guideline. Thanks to the faithfulness of our readers in reporting such finds, it would be rare (though not entirely impossible) to find an authentic, previously undiscovered item that by now we have not shown, so be extremely suspicious.

Even today, dinnerware companies continue to produce lines that draw on Fiesta's Art Deco appeal. In Plate 230 is a line by Mikasa called Moderna, designed by Larry Laslo. Note the ring handles on the cups and the sugar bowl. This line was carried by some of the larger mail-order firms in 1985 and '86. It was available in several colors; each piece is marked Mikasa. White 'Fiesta' is featured in restaurants located in Rockefeller Center by Restaurant Associates who commissioned Rego China of Whitestone, Queens, to make the ware for them. Nineteen pieces were designed; and although none of the original molds were used, the style is unmistakable.

Plate 230

Plate 231

Plate 232

A very curious pitcher has been reported to us three times over the past several years. It is a standard ball jug shape in solid colors (the photos that were sent in showed one in white, another in cobalt, and the third one in gray-blue). The question it raised was in regard to the mark it carried in each instance. It is marked with a large, ink-stamped F in script with an R in a circle to the right of the F's curving top bar. Under the F is the puzzling indication: Fiesta, USA — however, in an entirely different lettering style than Homer Laughlin's.

Other HLC look-alikes in Plates 231 include a bud vase with an obviously inferior glaze; it's just enough smaller to indicate that it has been cast from a mold made from an original vase. The little disk pitcher is not from a child's set of Fiesta, even though its color and design suggest that it might well be. The cobalt pitcher looks very much like the Harlequin novelty creamer, but it has no band of rings. The donkey may look like its Harlequin double but sometimes pulls a cart marked 'California.'

In Plate 232 you'll see a refrigerator jar that looks very much like the KK stacking unit in color as well as weight, though it is much smaller in size. We haven't a clue as to its manufacturer. There are bulb-type candle holders very similar to Fiesta's and salt and pepper shakers of many types. One curious set we once saw consisted of what appeared to be a genuine Fiesta salt shaker perched atop a little raised platform with handles which was actually the pepper. HLC had never heard of it. And have you seen the pie plate with Harlequin-like rings? We've seen examples in cobalt and light green, and the colors match HLC's glazes perfectly. Our Homer Laughlin contact assured us that they were not Harlequin, nor were they produced by them for any other market. But you'll have a hard time convincing collectors of this, and since we were misinformed (unintentionally, I'm sure) concerning a few other pieces we asked about, that may well be the case here.

So be cautious. We welcome your inquiries if you have questions concerning identification. If there are new discoveries — and there may yet be — we will do our best to keep you informed and up to date.

THE MORGUE

Several years ago on one of our visits to HLC, we were allowed a rare treat — a visit to the dark, secretive room hidden behind a locked and barred door in the uppermost niche of the office building that somehow down through the years earned the name *the morgue*. Dark and dingy it may be, but to a collector of HLC dinnerware, it's filled with excitement! A Fantasy Island, if indeed one ever existed.

We were allowed to dig through boxes and shelves where we found fantastic experimentals, beautiful trial glazes, and unfamiliar modifications of more standard forms. On our second visit some years later, we returned with a professional photographer through whose photos we are able to share the fun with all of you.

In Plate 233, left to right, is a divided relish molded in one piece; it measures 11" in diameter and has the look of Fiesta. The carafe, 10" tall, was sold with another HLC line; but this particular example was for some unknown reason dipped in the light green of the colored dinnerware lines we love. In the center is a magnificent Fiesta red 12" vase over which wars would certainly be waged if it were up for grabs — which, we must stress, it is *not*, nor are any of these other fabulous pieces; so please don't even ask! They are all company property and will remain so. There is a museum at the factory outlet in Newell where some of them are now on display. The piece to the right of the vase looks very familiar except for its size. It's 6½" tall, scaled to perfection to match the Fiesta syrup. Directly in front of it is the only marked piece we saw in the morgue. Most experimentals were merely marked with a number or not at all. This one, however, was embossed 'Fiesta' in the mold. It's 5" across by 1" deep and has the band of rings on the flange. The green relish section on the right was designed so that four would fit a large oval wooden tray. The coffee mug in yellow is 3" high and except for the short tapered base is exactly like the standard mug.

Plate 233

133

One of the most beautiful and exciting pieces of the Fiesta experimentals we know you'll enjoy seeing is the individual teapot shown in Plate 234. It is 6" high, and the lid is interchangeable with the demitasse pot. It was one of several pieces modeled by Fredrick Rhead, the designer, that was never marketed due to the onset of the war — in fact, many already existing lines had to be cut back. Though this teapot was never mass produced, at least three (all in ivory) have been accounted for.

In Plate 235, you'll see two adaptations of some standard Fiesta pieces. The French casserole is a footed version of the more familiar yellow one. The bowl measures 9¾" tall by 6" across; the high foot that has been added here nicely transforms a rather utilitarian mixing bowl into an elegant serving piece.

One item we especially liked on our first trip through the morgue was a vase that was out on loan when we made our return visit. We've yet to have the opportunity to photograph it ourselves, but we'll try to describe it for you. It was glazed in ivory with a 6" upright disk body that looked like the joined front halves of two juice pitchers without their ice guards.

There was a stack of Fiesta plates in unbelievable trial glazes — a pink beige, a spatter effect in dark brown on orange, a smoky delphinium blue, a dark red grape that might possibly be the rose ebony referred to in Rhead's article, a dark russet, a deep mustard yellow, and our favorite — black with four chromium bands.

Harlequin experimentals are shown in Plate 236. The nappy is 4" across and is shaped like the small Fiesta fruits. Next, a sauce cup, perhaps, made from the demitasse cup mold. The deep dish in mauve blue is 2½" x 7"— it has the Harlequin rings inside. On the far right, the yellow bowl measures 2½" by 5½" in diameter.

Other goodies that were out on loan during our second visit were two different styles of Harlequin candle holders that we had catalogued before. One pair was large and flat, 5½" in diameter with a 2½" tall candle cup in the center. The others were shaped like the large half of an inverted cone, 4¼" across the bottom and 3" tall. Both styles were lovely, but not quite as nice as our regular Harlequin candle holders.

One of the most exciting of the Harlequin pieces we saw was a demitasse cup and saucer in a beautiful high-gloss black. Trial glaze plates included light chocolate, deep gray, delphinium blue, vanilla, caramel, black, and a luscious lavender.

The tall 6" Riviera candle holders we had fallen in love with were also on loan, but the footed console bowl was there for our photography session. (See Plate 237.) It's huge! 3½" x 8½" x 13½" long! The ivory Century piece is a one-piece fast-stand sauce dish, 7" across the attached tray. A collector recently reported that she found one of these in a mall in Oklahoma! Although the butter dish on the right is just the size to hold a quarter-pound stick of today's butter, it was the only one of the three sizes never marketed. This one is 7½" long.

We hope you have found this peek inside the morgue to be as much fun as it was for us to bring it to you. It is strictly off-limits to the public, and we appreciate the opportunity of photographing these lovely experimentals for you to see.

Plate 234

Plate 235

Plate 236

Plate 237

EXPERIMENTALS AND EMPLOYEES' INVENTIONS

In addition to the experimentals from the morgue, a few more very rare or one-of-a-kind items have been found outside the factory. Those that were made from a specifically-designed mold or glazed in a trial color we call experimentals; those that were glazed in non-regulation glazes or items that were put together at the whim of an inventive employee, we'll call employees' inventions.

Plate 238 shows our regular two-pint jug alongside another that holds just one pint. This is the only one we've heard of and really have no information whatsoever on it. The Harlequin tumbler in Plate 239 has been fitted with a Riviera handle — a one-of-a-kind employees' invention. Plates 240 through 245 are experimentals. The 10" compote is a scaled-down model of our 12" version. There are at least three collectors who have been lucky enough to find one of these. Alongside the standard onion soup in Plate 242 is (as far as we know) a one-of-a-kind variation that was undiscovered until only a few years ago. Shown here in light green, it differs from the regular version in several ways: note that the handles are flat rather than rolled under, the bowl flares at the rim above the handles, and the foot is wider and shorter. The lid is less rounded and ½" wider. It's marked 'Fiesta HLC' in the mold.

Plate 240 contains a unique creamer and sugar bowl on the standard figure-8 tray. This set and another creamer have been found in ivory, and the same sugar bowl is shown in Plate 246 in a near-Wells Art Glaze brown. (Photography © Adam Anik)

Plate 238

Plate 239

Plate 240

Plate 241

Plate 242

Plate 243

Plate 244

Plate 246

Plate 245

There are three distinct differences between the sugar bowls in Plate 243 (the experimental is on the left, the standard sugar bowl on the right): 1) the base is raised and the inside bottom flat; 2) the width of the lip flange is twice as wide; and 3) the mark is Fiesta HLC, USA. This is the same mark that you'll find on the stick-handled creamer; another similarity to that piece is the flat inside bottom. The owner of this rare item says he believes this to be a very early design, possibly modeled as a companion to the stick-handled creamer, later modified to eliminate possible production problems.

The red 6" tray shown in Plate 244 was purchased several years ago in the Newell, West Virginia, area. The seller had used it under the syrup pitcher, saying that it fit perfectly. As you can see just by the photos in this chapter, most of these one-of-a-kind (or at least extremely limited) items have been found in ivory, and most are unmarked. So this piece is very unusual, not only in its rarity but also because of the red glaze; and, to top it all off, it is marked Fiesta in the mold.

The collectors who sent the bowl in Plate 245 like to call this item a 'spaghetti bowl.' It is shown in a relish base for comparison. Under the flange on the outside is the familiar band of rings. This piece is 1⅜" deep and 10⅞" in diameter. It's unmarked, but unmistakably Fiesta.

'Ingenious' is the best way to describe the candle holder in Plate 247. It's made from the stem of a sweets compote, a demitasse saucer, and of course you recognize the familiar Fiesta ring handle. Plate 248 shows a pair of sherbets, unproduced though clearly marked in the mold, in swirling pastel glazes. (Both photos © Adam Anik)

The test plate shown in Plate 249 is dated 1929 and shows a variety of color samples as well as various decals. Items such as these are treasured very highly by collectors. Plates 250 through 252 are standard items in non-regulation glazes. The 4¾" fruit bowl is in Skytone blue, a color used in several of their other dinnerware lines from the fifties. The Tom and Jerry mug is one from a punch set containing twelve mugs and a large salad bowl, all in maroon. The set has been broken up now, and each mug (when one hits the market) is snapped up at a premium price. The mint green 9" plate was a trial glaze — it bears a handwritten, underglaze identification code of '5971.' Its owner describes it as 'somewhere between light green and turquoise.'

Plate 247

Plate 248

Plate 249

Plate 250

Plate 251

Plate 252

Plate 253

Plate 254

Plate 256

Plate 255

The lamps in Plates 253 and 256 are made with Fiesta and Harlequin components. The body of the large cobalt lamp was fabricated from two Harlequin casseroles; the neck is a Fiesta sweets comport stem, and the base is the Fiesta fruit bowl. The Fiesta lamp was made from casserole bases; again the neck is a sweets comport stem, and the base is a small fruit bowl. Both are excellent examples of what HLC's inventive employees could do. The boudoir lamps made from syrup bottoms (Plates 254 and 255) were more than likely assembled by another company and sold commercially, since there are several in existence and bases are nearly always identical. Both styles are sometimes found with hand-painted flowers. The cobalt Fiesta syrup-lamps have their original shades. The hand-painted yellow Harlequin lamp has an unusual marble base.

KITCHEN KRAFT AND OVEN-SERVE

From the very early 1930's, Homer Laughlin China was the leading manufacturer of a very successful type of oven-to-table kitchenware. These lines were called Oven-Serve and Kitchen Kraft. The variety of items offered and the many patterns and decaled lines that were made represent an endless field of interest for collectors today.

The extensive line with the tulip decals, examples of which are shown in Plate 257, is marked 'Kitchen Kraft, Oven-Serve.' You are sure to find more matching pieces. Shown is the casserole in the metal holder, cake plate, medium covered jar, stacking refrigerator set, salt and pepper shakers, and the pie server. (For a larger listing of available items, see 'Suggested Values' in the back of the book.)

It's nothing short of amazing how well this type of ware stands up to constant use. We knew of a lady who had used the same Kitchen Kraft pie plate for twenty years — at least once every week, she told us. The glaze looked as new as if it were just out of the store.

Plate 257

Various floral decaled Kitchen Kraft lines were produced, every one of them lovely. In Plates 258 through 261 you'll see several. The elusive underplate is shown in Plate 259 decorated with an unusual and very attractive decal — this is the only piece we've ever seen with this particular design; it measures 7" in diameter. The pie plate and matching platter (Plate 261) is from a line called Kitchen Bouquet, according to the backstamp.

The label reproduced below was found on a floral-embossed spoon and fork in the rust glaze; examples of this line are shown on page 144.

Guaranteed
To Withstand Changes of

Oven-Dinner Ware

"THE OVEN WARE FOR TABLE SERVICE"

The Homer Laughlin China Co.
Newell, W. Va.

Plate 258

Plate 259

Plate 260

Plate 261

In Plates 262 through 264 are examples of the line embossed with the same floral pattern that decorates the handles of the Fiesta Kitchen Kraft spoon, fork, and server. The custard set in the wire rack shows a variety of available colors; yellow and rust are the most commonly encountered, and you may also find a piece or two in dark green. Also shown is a rare batter pitcher in white, a hard-to-find color. Another decorative treatment (see Plate 262) utilizes brightly colored decals over the embossing. Shown here is the 2½-quart casserole and the underplate.

Plate 262

Plate 263

Plate 264

AMERICANA

This very attractive set was made exclusively for Montgomery Ward who offered it for sale in their catalogs from 1944 through 1956. Each piece (thirty-one in all) carries a different design patterned after Currier and Ives prints. The rose-pink decorations suggestive of mulberry historical Staffordshire ware were 'printed from fine copper engravings,' so states the ad in the 1944 catalog.

These pieces were available: cup and saucer; plates 10", 8½", 7", 6", and 8" square; dessert/fruit bowl; demitasse cup and saucer; coupe soup; creamer and sugar bowl with lid; sauce boat and stand; egg cup; teapot; oval platters 11", 13", 15"; round platter, 13"; oval vegetable bowl; round vegetable bowls 8", 9"; and vegetable bowl lid, 9".

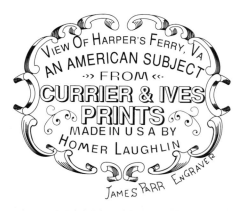

Plate 265

CENTURY

These are only a few examples of the many different decal decorations applied to Century shapes. You'll find that many carry the name of the line on the back, and the year of their manufacture is often indicated by a dating code. Some of the more attractive and accessible patterns are being reassembled by today's collectors.

One line, Sun Porch (represented by the teapot below), is novel in that the decal depicts pieces of Fiesta on the table under the umbrella (Photography © Adam Anik). It is interesting to note that this teapot is the only piece of Sun Porch ever found not in a Kitchen Kraft shape. There are bowls, a covered jar, a covered jug, a pie plate, and a cake plate, but all are Kitchen Kraft. The collector who has them tells us he believes that this is an earlier line than Fiesta and suspects that Rhead modeled the carafe and bulb candlesticks after this decal. English Garden is the name of the lovely dinnerware show in Plate 268. According to the backstamp, this line was made circa 1933. The casserole is marked with the Wells peacock trademark you see here. The Wells family became involved with the company as early as 1889 when William Edwin Wells became Homer Laughlin's partner. Succeeding generations continued as leaders of the firm. Note the inside decal on the casserole. Also shown are the egg cup, fast-stand gravy boat, plates 10" and 8", creamer and sugar bowl, butter dish, syrup jug with lid, and cream soup. Of special interest in this photo is the butter dish. This is actually the Century shape, one of only a few we've seen in all these years. The one used in combination with lines on Century in virtually every instance is the Jade butter dish; you'll see more of this shape on one of the following pages.

For years people with a bit of disdain for inexpensive depression-era dinnerware have said, 'Oh, they used to give that stuff away at the movies.' Well, here is a Century set that really was. Plates with the legend shown have turned up from several Northeastern states and from at least one Southern state. These pieces are never marked on the back, but they are unmistakably HLC. In Plate 269 you'll see a 6" plate, cup and saucer, deep plate, luncheon plate, and fruit bowl. (Photography © Adam Anik)

Plate 266

Plate 267

Plate 268

Plate 269

CHILDREN'S SETS

Children's sets were not made in great numbers; they're hard to find and make very desirable additions to any collection. Borrowing a plate from the Century line, the Dick Tracy set is rare and very collectible both as a HLC child's set and as an example of character memorabilia. These are especially sought after, collectors tell us, in the California area due to the popularity of collectibles pertaining to the movie industry.

The child's bowl below is decorated with the familiar green and white checks of the Ralston Purina Company; these were made by HLC as premiums for Ralston customers. The very exciting set in Plate 273, as you can see, utilizes the Fiesta molds. The same comic animal decals may also be found on the shapes used for the Tom and the Butterfly set shown below. You'll find some of these marked with an ink-stamped series of letters and numbers. For help in deciphering these codes, see the section called 'Dating Codes and English Measurements.'

Plate 270

Plate 271

148

Plate 272

Plate 273

DOGWOOD

Dogwood is an especially lovely line of HLC dinnerware that was produced in the early 1960s. At least twenty items were made; see 'Suggested Values' in the back of the book for a complete listing. Included were five sizes of plates. Among the harder-to-find items in this pattern are the 8" salad plate, the 10" dinner plate, the teapot, and the Kitchen Kraft mixing bowl set. The Dogwood decal has also been reported on Rhythm shapes.

Plate 274

Plate 275

HARMONY LINES

The Kitchen Kraft below is decorated in an Art Deco leaf pattern, one of the Harmony lines we told you about in the chapter entitled 'The Story of Fiesta.' This line was undiscovered until the sixth edition, and we were doubly excited to learn that a matching line of Kitchen Kraft had been produced. This, of course, is the line that coordinated with red Fiesta; in Plate 276 you'll see the casserole, mixing bowl, pie plate, spoon, fork, and server. More pieces are shown in Plate 277; represented along with the Kitchen Kraft jar are these Nautilus pieces: lug cereal/soup bowl, 6½" and 7½" plates, cup and saucer, creamer and sugar bowl, and large vegetable bowl. It is interesting to note that collectors report finding several more Nautilus items than those that are listed in the Harmony assortment on page 10.

A second Harmony line (Plate 278) was designed to go with Fiesta yellow. Collectors have termed this pattern 'Shaggy Flower.' Shown are a Nautilus cup with a Fiesta saucer, Kitchen Kraft individual casserole, Nautilus fruit bowl and 6½" plate, 7½" Fiesta plate, Kitchen Kraft shakers and jug with a yellow lid. (Photography in Plates 277 and 278 © Adam Anik)

Plate 276

Plate 277

Plate 278

HISTORICAL AMERICAN SUBJECTS

Produced for the F. W. Woolworth Company who sold it though their retail stores, Historical American Subjects was aptly named. At least nineteen pieces were made, each decorated with scenes reproduced from the original works of Joseph Boggs Beale. All that has been reported to us has been in the rose-pink as shown here except for the 8" plate which has also been found in blue. The line, as far as we know, consisted of plates 10", 9", 8", and 7"; rim soup, 8½"; dessert/fruit bowl, 5¾"; platters 13" and 11"; round and oval vegetable bowls, 8¾" and 9½"; cup and saucer; cereal/soup bowl; creamer and sugar bowl, teapot, gravy boat and undertray. Scenes bear titles such as 'Betsy Ross and the Flag,' 'Lincoln's Gettysburg Address,' 'George Washington Taking Command of the Army,' 'The First Thanksgiving,' and 'Paul Revere.' Though very hard to find, there's lots of enthusiasm for this line, and prices are already higher than for most decaled dinnerware.

Plate 279

153

JADE

The pattern shown here is La Hacienda; the shape is called Jade. According to the dating code in the backstamp, it was made circa 1935. Though we always thought the stick butter dishes were on the Century shape because they were consistently found in Century-based Mexican lines (their styling is extremely compatible with them), here's proof that indeed they belong to the Jade line. Only the round butter dish shown in the Hacienda section (and again in Century/English Garden) is actually a Century butter.

Plate 280 includes a 11" platter (a Century shape), 9" plate, gravy boat and liner, casserole, creamer and sugar bowl. Note the finials and the shape of the gravy liner. This line is very rare.

Plate 280

NAUTILUS

Here's the Nautilus shape again — it was shown in the Mexican lines and again as a basis for two of the Harmony lines. This time the pattern is called Old Curiosity Shop; though very hard to find, it has lots of charm and is sought after by HLC's dinnerware collectors. Shown is the cup and saucer, 6½" plate, deep bowl, casserole with lid, fruit bowl, 11½" platter, deep plate, 9½" plate, gravy boat and liner, butter dish (Jade shape), and creamer and sugar bowl. (Photography © Adam Anik)

Plate 281

PRISCILLA

This is one of the many beautiful patterns of dinnerware fast becoming very collectible. It's an extensive line and relatively easy to find. Two styles were produced; the regular line, simple round shapes on Eggshell (their lightweight semi-porcelain), and a second line that utilized the Republic shape. Both are shown below. In addition to the dinnerware, you'll find matching Kitchen Kraft. Among the harder-to-find items are the tall teapot (shape designation unknown) shown in Plate 282 to the far left, the Republic teapot, and these Kitchen Kraft items: the 9½" fruit bowl (far right), coffeepot, and the tab-handled platter. A more complete listing is offered in the 'Suggested Values' section.

Plate 282

Plate 283

Plate 282
    Tall Teapot; Deep Plate, 8½"; Plates, 10" (the second is Republic**); Kitchen Kraft Fruit Bowl; Republic Creamer and Sugar Bowl, and Republic Teapot.**

Plate 283
    Kitchen Kraft Jug, Coffeepot, Mixing Bowls, and Casserole; Regular Teapot, and Republic Teapot.

RHYTHM

Rhythm is a shape designed by Don Schreckengost. We're most familiar with it as one of the colored dinnerware lines, of course, but it was the basis of several decaled lines as well. While we once thought the Western dinnerware shown in Plate 284 was a child's set, we've since heard from a lady who received some as a wedding gift. She tells us there were serving pieces such as a creamer and sugar bowl, vegetable bowls, and platter, and from another source we've learned that there was even an ash tray to match.

American Provincial is the name of the decal on the spoon rest, and the lovely floral in Plate 286 is called Rhythm Rose. It was produced from the mid-40s through the mid-50s and is marked with the gold stamp: Household Institute, Rhythm Rose.

Plate 284

Plate 285

Plate 286

SWING

Swing, introduced in 1938, was the first of HLC's shapes in the Eggshell weight. By '45 it was identified only as Eggshell, not to be confused with Eggshell Nautilus, a lighter-weight version of the Nautilus shape, or Eggshell Georgian, a lightweight rendering of a classic English shape.

This line was decaled and/or pastel-striped and included a wide variety of pieces allowing for such unusual (for HLC) presentations as a breakfast-in-bed set. The shakers were also used with Virginia Rose and Rhythm.

Because of its delicate appearance, pastels and floral treatments abound. And, on rare occasions, you may find it in the Hacienda pattern, in blue-trimmed Mexicana, in Conchita, and in Mexicali.

Two lovely floral-decorated casseroles are shown in Plate 287 (Photography © Adam Anik). Plate 288 contains what we once thought to be a child's set; it's actually an After Dinner (or Breakfast-in-Bed) creamer, cup and saucer, and a 6" plate. The plate (bottom right) is from an appealing dinnerware line called Colonial Kitchen. Another line that has been reported to us is Chinese Green Goddess. The decal is a large orange covered urn, tall yellow vase, bowl and jugs, a green turtle, and the green goddess on a black pedestal. And on the Eggshell Swing you may find a pattern stamped (on the back) Pueblo with a bare-breasted Indian woman making clay pots on a multicolored rug. For a complete listing of available items, see 'Suggested Values.'

HLC ©
SWING
Eggshell
U·S·A
138 N 5

Plate 287

Plate 288

Plate 289

VIRGINIA ROSE

Virginia Rose was the name given a line of standard HLC shapes which from 1929 until the early 1970s was used as the basis for more than a dozen patterns of decaled or embossed dinnerware. The designer was Fredrick Rhead; and the name was chosen in honor of the daughter of Joseph Mahan Wells, grand-daughter of Wm. E. Wells. Virginia Rose was one of the most popular shapes ever produced. Even after it was discontinued for use in the home, the shape was adopted by the hotel china division at HLC and became a bestseller in the field of hotel and institutional ware. Shown here is only a sampling of the many floral patterns you may find on pieces marked Virginia Rose. You may find other pieces. (For a more complete listing of available items, see 'Suggested Values' in the back of the book.)

Plate 290

Plate 291

Among the harder-to-find items in the dinnerware line are the double egg cup, coffee mug, 8" tray with handles, and the salt and pepper shakers. A matching line of Kitchen Kraft is also available, some of it is limited as well. The 12" pie plate, salt and pepper shakers, cake plate and server, straight-sided casserole, and the 8" casserole with round sides are scarce.

Plate 292

Plate 293

Plate 290
Plates, Soups, Salt and Pepper Shakers, Egg Cup, Oatmeal, Deep Bowl. Two styles of 8" soups are shown here. The one on the left has a 1" wide flange, while the type on the right has none. The plates measure 10", 8", and 6"; the small oatmeal is 6", and the deep bowl is 5".

Plate 291
Kitchen Kraft Salt and Pepper Shakers and Casserole; 8" Tray. The straight-sided casserole is harder to find than the one shown in Plate 292. The small tray may have been used alone as a serving piece or as an undertray for the casserole. It's very scarce.

Plate 292
Covered Vegetable, Cake Set, Platters, Plate, Sauce Boat, Butter Dish, Creamer and Sugar, Cup and Saucer, Casserole. This is the 15" platter, the 8" plate, and the 8" Kitchen Kraft casserole. The 9½" platter is used here as the sauce boat liner.

Plate 293
Water Pitcher, Milk Pitcher, Kitchen Kraft Mixing Bowls. The water pitcher measures 7½"; the milk pitcher, 5".

LAUGHLIN ART CHINA

In the early 1900s in an attempt to enter the art pottery field, HLC produced a unique line of art china. It was marked in gold or black with an eagle and the name 'Laughlin Art China.' Examples of this ware are very rare, but it has an enthusiastic following. Many more photos than what we have room to show you here were submitted for this edition; those we can't show you, we'll try to describe.

Perhaps as many as eighty-nine shapes were used, and several decorating techniques were employed. Most are decaled, but occasionally you will find a hand-decorated piece that may be artist signed. Their most extensive pattern was called 'Currant,' brown ware with decals of berries and vines.

Many lovely pieces are shown in Plates 294 through 303 and again in Plate 306. Below are the 2" x 10" ruffled salad bowl, the 9½" plaque, and the 10" scalloped plate. In the next photograph, you'll see a very rare 6" humidor, a 6" bulbous pitcher, the 'orange' bowl with handles (it measures 12" across), and the straight-sided 6½" pitcher. Plate 296 contains a 6½" x 12" 'Fe Dora' bread tray, and below that a breathtaking demitasse set. At the bottom of the page is a 7" vase, a very rare, large covered casserole, and a 10" pitcher the company called 'Dutch Jug.' Plate 301 displays several lovely and very rare pieces: 9¾", 12", and 16" vases, and a chocolate or after dinner pot in a second style. It's 10" tall. Two large vases appear in Plates 302 and 303 — a 14" one with handles and another that measures 12½".

Plate 294

Plate 295

Two unique items are shown in Plate 306, one of them is Currant. These are called sugar baskets. The gold-trimmed one is from a line called 'Golden Fleece.'

In addition to the Currant shown in the color plates, you may also find a small stein, an 8" vase with small round handles at the rim and a body that widens toward the base, a handled cake plate, an odd-shaped bowl ruffled on one side with a handle on the other, and a shallow, ruffled piece with a spout and a handle the owner thinks might be a sauce boat of some sort. There's a humidor, nut dishes with and without handles, and several other pieces we've not yet shown. If we can get photos, we'll try to include more of this elusive line in the next edition.

A few pieces have been found decorated in flow blue with gold trim and decals of children in period costume; you'll see a cup and saucer in Plate 304 and a 7" 3-part candy dish to the right. Plate 308 contains a lady's cuspidor in flow blue and gold. It measures 5½" x 8½", and in the last edition we included a flow blue jardiniere (10" x 14½") trimmed in gold with handles and a decal of a child. The vase in the middle is 12" tall. There's a peacock in the background, and it features a lovely Nouveau-style lady. Monks were often used on mugs and steins, and you may find the tall tankard decorated with a decal very similar to the one on the small mug shown in Plate 308.

Plate 296

Plate 297

Plate 299

Plate 300

Plate 298

162

Plate 301

Plate 302

Plate 303

'White Pets' is the name of the line shown in Plate 307. This is a milk pitcher; the flaking you see in the picture is common. These pieces are hand painted, though they may be painted over a decal. Occasionally you will find one bearing an artist's signature. Other reported pieces include a handled 8" vase and a small stein.

In the last edition we showed a 10" plate in the same pattern as the tankard and mug set in Plate 309. The plate was marked with the line name, 'An American Beauty, Semi-Vitreous China, 1900.' The tall tankard shown here is decorated on the back with a second lady's portrait. Items such as these are extremely rare; a complete set like this one would be next to impossible to reassemble.

Plates 310 and 311 contain a pitcher decorated with plums and a tall floral tankard marked 'American Floral.' They're the only examples we're aware of with these particular designs. The small steins in Plates 312 and 313 are unusual examples on one of the more commonly-found shapes. The one with the football player is inscribed 'Copyright 1905 by the H. M. Suter Publishing Company'; the name John E. Sheridan is signed on a diagonal near the player's elbow. The second stein was commissioned by a hardware company. It reads 'Berger Manufacturing Company Souvenir Mug, Canton, Ohio, Everything in Sheet Metal' on the front, and on the back 'Ohio Hardware Association, February 27, 1928.' We've also seen these mugs with a multicolored Jacobean design that is very attractive.

Plate 304

Plate 305

Plate 306

Plate 307

Plate 308

Plate 309

Plate 310

Plate 311

Plate 312

Plate 313

Laughlin's Dreamland

Children feeding a pet goat, doing laundry, playing badminton and crying when their dog steals the 'birdie' decorate this winsome but rare line made by Homer Laughlin in the early years after the turn of the century. It appears to be done in a technique called pouncing that was used by several of the larger art pottery manufacturers who operated in the same general area. Plate 314 contains a wonderful tankard set on shapes that we have seen before marked Laughlin Art China; another Art China shape is in Plate 316 — the ruffled salad bowl. The little jug measures 6½", and the tiny vase in the bottom left-hand corner is a mere 3½". Two platters have also been reported: 10" and 12", the latter described as having a scalloped, scrolled rim, a humidor, a handled nut dish, and a mug. It will be interesting to see what other examples crop up.

Plate 314

Plate 315

Plate 316

167

Plate 317

In the photo above is the piece referred to by Homer Laughlin as their 'orange bowl.' This time it is decorated (again by pouncing) with a scene of three Dutch children watching a mother duck and her ducklings waddle by. The stamp on the bottom of the bowl identifies this line as 'Laughlin's Holland.' This is the only piece ever reported to us in this pattern.

Plate 318

Since we first showed this piece, we've received a confirmation of its mark — Genesee, which is the name of a standard company shape used as early as the 1910s. The collector who shared this information with us has three 6½" plates, all showing children engaged in various activities. These had been in her family and used by her mother when she was a child, probably before 1920. In addition to the small plates, she also has the same designs on an 8" coupe soup bowl, a 3¾" wide cup, and a 5" fruit bowl. These full-size pieces are marked 'Empress,' another early shape name, not a pattern.

WORLD'S FAIR
THE AMERICAN POTTER

As a tribute to the American Potter, six pottery companies united their efforts and jointly built and operated an actual working kiln at the 1939– '40 World's Fair in New York. A variety of plates, vases, figural items, and bowls were produced and marked with an ink stamp 'The American Potter, 1939 (or '40), World's Fair Exhibit, Joint Exhibit of Capital and Labor.' The Homer Laughlin China Company entry, designed by Fredrick Rhead, is shown in Plate 321. In the center of each plate, you can see the Trylon and Parisphere, adopted symbols of the Fair. One of these plates has been found with this commemorative message stamped in gold on the back: 'Decorated by Charles Murphy, 150th Anniversary Inauguration of George Washington as First President of the United States, 1789-1939.'

In Plate 319 are the entries from the other five companies. Left to right: Cake set, 'Cronin China Co., Minerva O., National Brotherhood of Operative Potters,' Bowl, 'Paden City Pottery, Made in USA,' 10"; Plate, 'Knowles, Joint Exhibit of Capital and Labor,' 10¾"; Marmalade bottom, embossed with Trylon and Parisphere and 'New York World's Fair,' marked 'Edwin M. Knowles China Co., Semi-Vitreous,' 3"; Pitcher, marked 'Porcelier Trade Mark, Vitreous Hand Decorated China, Made in U.S.A.'

The plates and ash tray in Plate 320 are souvenirs of the Golden Gate International Exposition of 1939 and 1940. They are marked 'Golden Gate Intern. Expo., Copyright License 63C, Homer Laughlin, Souvenir.' Below them are the plates designed by Rhead for the New York World's Fair.

Though the George and Martha pitchers in Plate 322 are shown here in cobalt, they're much more readily available in ivory. Martha is marked 'The American Potter, New York World's Fair' with the year 1940 on a raised disk superimposed over a Trylon. George is marked 'First Edition For Collectors, New York's World's Fair, 1939.' He has also been found with this mark: 'Joint Exhibition of Capital and Labor, American Potter, NY WF, 1939.' These measure 5" tall; you'll find smaller examples about 2" in height. They're sometimes in a bisque finish, and examples in mauve blue and Harlequin yellow have been reported. They sometimes appear as salt and pepper shakers or toothpick holders. These are usually not marked.

Plate 319

169

The Four Season plates in Plate 323 each measure 4¼" in diameter. Spring shows a man fishing for trout; Summer depicts a family picnicking; a man hunting with his dog represents Autumn; and the Winter plate has a skating scene. These sets are usually found in the colors shown, but a set in turquoise has been reported.

We show only one (Plate 324), but you'll find vases in many colors, sizes, and shapes that were hand turned at the fair. They're usually in the 1½" to 7" range, and all are ink stamped 'American Potter.' Other items may also be found; in earlier editions we've shown a candle holder and a Harlequin individual creamer with 'World's Fair' etched on its side.

The Potters' Plates shown in Plate 325 are possibly the easiest of the World's Fair items to find. There were two; The Potter at His Wheel and The Artist Decorating the Vase. They have been found in turquoise as shown here and in light green; they're scarce in light green and ivory. We've seen one in a dark mocha marked 'First Edition For Collectors Limited to 100 Pieces, #85.' Shown with the plates is a cup and saucer embossed with signs of the Zodiac — another rarity.

Plate 320

Plate 321

Plate 322

Plate 323

Plate 324

Plate 325

MISCELLANEOUS

Here are a few last items of interest we wanted to share with you. Below is a Sit'n Sip set in the original carton. These were marketed during the late sixties into the early seventies. Most, though not all, carry advertising messages. The same type of mug set is being offered in gift stores today; now we're instructed to keep our coffee hot longer by using the coaster as a lid.

The nude vases and the donkey ash tray (Plate 327) are glazed in Fiesta red and ivory. One of the vases is marked by hand under the glaze 'GAW,' more than likely the initials of is creator. All three of these pieces were discovered near Newell, WV, the property of an HLC supervisor. We've seen a photograph of a green donkey ashtray and a mauve blue donkey figurine. The owner has two small vases she believes are HLC as well, identical in form (pilgrim flask shapes with angle handles), one in the red and the second in the mauve blue glaze. Both are commemoratives. She suspects that a spruce monkey figurine she once had came from HLC, too. Does anyone have any information concerning these items?

Shown in Plate 328 is a football trophy designed by an HLC employee in the early forties to commemorate Bill Booth, an Ohio State football star from East Liverpool (notice the 'O' on his jersey). Booth was tragically killed in an automobile accident, and a very limited number of these trophies were dipped in the Fiesta glazes to present to his teammates. Besides the light green one shown there, a yellow one is on display along with other Fiesta experimental and production pieces at the Homer Laughlin factory, and we have reports of an ivory one. (Photography by Linda Saridakis)

The last just-for-fun photo shows a prized piece of needlepoint and the setup of Fiesta that it represents so well. This is a lovely item made for a pair of avid Fiesta collectors by a member of their family — we thought you might enjoy seeing it.

Plate 326

Plate 327

Plate 328

Plate 329

SUGGESTED VALUES

Values are suggested for items that are in mint condition – that is to say no chip, 'chigger bites,' or 'dings'! The three sagger pin marks that are evident on the underside of many pieces are characteristic and result from the technique employed in stacking the ware for firing. These should in no way be considered damage. Slightly scratched items are usually worth about 30% below 'book'; those with heavy scratches or tiny 'dings' on areas where the damage is obvious should sell for approximately 50% to 60% below. One should learn to grade merchandise carefully and to adjust prices accordingly. Don't expect to get book price for worn or otherwise inferior items.

Decals when present must be complete, the colors well preserved, with very little wear. When decals are worn, faded, or otherwise appear to be in less-than-mint condition, items should be evaluated following the above guidelines.

When buying odd lids and bases, remember that glaze colors vary; and some lids and openings will be just enough off-round that they will not fit properly. If you do buy them separately, expect to pay 50% to 60% of listed values for lids and 40% to 50% for bases. For example, if a sugar bowl is listed at $20.00, its lid would be approximately $10.00 to $12.00 and its base $8.00 to $10.00.

Fiesta
See Plates 1 through 43

The first column of figures represents the range of values suggested for these colors: red, cobalt, and ivory; the second column contains values for turquoise, yellow, and light green. Medium green continues to appreciate rapidly, and the colors of the fifties are climbing steadily as well. In the last edition, rose and gray were the prefered 'Fifties Colors,' but the trend now seems to be reversing. Until the dust has settled, you'll have to be the judge.

As has always been our practice, to arrive at these evaluations we conducted a survey of dealers and collectors representing the North, South, East, and West of our country. Again, as is always the case, we found that their opinions were widely varied, but we tried to be fair and unbiased as we interpreted the figures before us. There were some respondents who reported on the market in their areas where prices are considerably higher than the figures we ultimately arrived at. We were entreated by another to 'go back to 1994 prices — Fiesta has become overpriced, and we find it slow to sell at 'book value' and hard to buy for resale.' So we often had a very broad range of values to average; but our function in this is simply to interpret. We have nothing to gain by manipulating the outcome of our survey, since we no longer buy or sell Fiesta ourselves. So as we prepare our averages, we purposely shuffle the reports that have been sent in so we have no idea whose estimate we're looking at. Following the methods we've always used, we threw out the high and low estimates and averaged the others. Figures were never rounded off more than one dollar in either direction. What we arrived at we feel represents a high average. Please keep in mind that when we say 'high average' we mean that in most parts of the country, these might very likely be the 'asking' prices of dealers who specialize, carry a large stock, and sell only quality merchandise. As we all know, if we're willing to expend the effort to seek them out, there are always bargains to be had from other, less convenient resources. We're not trying to set your prices, and you may have to adjust them up or down according to what the market will bear in your area or selling arena.

There are fine points to collecting and price assessing that must be left up to the collector, since much of it is a matter of individual preference. Some collectors search out the medium green individual salad bowls that have no inside rings and the medium green cups that do and are willing to pay a premium to get them. Others find the issue to be of little consequence. So because a price guide can be only a general interpretation of the market, we'll leave those fine points up to the individual, though we have tried to make you aware of the fact that those subtle variations exist.

You'll notice on the following page that certain items are marked with an asterisk. This is to draw you attention to the fact that those particular items in the turquoise glaze were produced in a time span shorter by at least one year than the same items in the other original colors, since turquoise was not introduced until mid-1937, more than a year after the line was introduced. These are only the items that were dropped by 1946. There is a school of thought developing among collectors that because of the shorter time frame, these turquoise items are in less supply and therefore their prices should be higher. Do you agree? How much higher? You tell us. God willing, we will be doing another price update in the fall of 1997.

You are alway welcome to write us with your ideas and to report new developments and new finds. Our address is 1202 Seventh St., Covington, Indiana 47932. Or you can call us at (317) 793-2392, which is also our FAX number.

Fiesta

	Red/Cobalt, Ivory	Yellow, Turq., Lt. Green	Flfties Colors	Medium Green	As Shown/ Specified
Ashtray	40.00-50.00	35.00-42.00	65.00-75.00	120.00-140.00	
Bowl, covered onion soup					
in cobalt and ivory					500.00-550.00
in red					550.00-600.00
in turquoise					2,000.00-2,200.00
in yellow & lt. green					425.00-465.00
Bowl, cream soup	45.00-55.00	35.00-40.00	60.00-70.00	2,800.00-3,200.00	
Bowl, dessert; 6"	42.00-48.00	30.00-35.00	40.00-48.00	300.00-325.00	
Bowl, footed salad*	245.00-275.00	190.00-220.00			
Bowl, fruit; 11¾"*	215.00-235.00	170.00-190.00			
Bowl, fruit; 4¾"	25.00-30.00	20.00-24.00	28.00-32.00	335.00-375.00	
Bowl, fruit; 5½"	28.00-32.00	20.00-25.00	30.00-35.00	50.00-65.00	
Bowl, individual salad,					
in red, turquoise, or yellow, 7½"					65.00-75.00
in medium green, 7½"					75.00-95.00
Bowl, mixing; #1*	135.00-150.00	120.00-130.00			
Bowl, mixing; #2*	85.00-100.00	75.00-85.00			
Bowl, mixing; #3*	90.00-110.00	80.00-95.00			
Bowl, mixing; #4*	100.00-125.00	95.00-110.00			
Bowl, mixing; #5*	125.00-145.00	110.00-130.00			
Bowl, mixing; #6*	165.00-185.00	145.00-165.00			
Bowl, mixing; #7*	235.00-260.00	200.00-220.00			
Bowl, nappy, 8½"*	35.00-45.00	25.00-35.00	40.00-50.00	90.00-110.00	
Bowl, nappy, 9½"*	50.00-60.00	40.00-48.00			
Bowl, unlisted salad					
in yellow					80.00-90.00
in ivory, red, or cobalt					280.00-310.00
Candle holders, bulb; pr.*	90.00-110.00	75.00-85.00			
Candle holders, tripod; pr.*	460.00-485.00	365.00-385.00			
Carafe*	200.00-225.00	160.00-180.00			
Casserole	160.00-180.00	110.00-125.00	240.00-265.00	450.00-500.00	
Casserole, French; in yellow					220.00-245.00
in other standard color					425.00-475.00
Casserole, promotional;					
any color, complete					120.00-140.00
Coffeepot	190.00-210.00	145.00-165.00	245.00-265.00		
in gray					325.00-350.00
Coffeepot, demitasse*	275.00-300.00	225.00-250.00			
Comport, 12"*	145.00-165.00	115.00-130.00			
Comport, sweets*	70.00-80.00	60.00-68.00			
Creamer	22.00-28.00	15.00-20.00	30.00-38.00	58.00-68.00	
Creamer, individual; in red					175.00-200.00
in turquoise					270.00-295.00
in yellow					50.00-60.00
Creamer, stick-handled*	40.00-50.00	32.00-38.00			
Cup, demitasse	52.00-62.00	48.00-56.00	250.00-270.00		
Cup, see teacup					
Egg cup	50.00-60.00	45.00-50.00	125.00-145.00		
Lid for mixing bowl, #1–3					
any color					550.00-600.00
Lid for mixing bowl, #4					
any color					600.00-650.00
Marmalade*	200.00-225.00	170.00-190.00			
Mug, Tom and Jerry	65.00-75.00	45.00-55.00	80.00-90.00	90.00-105.00	
Mustard*	195.00-220.00	160.00-180.00			
Pitcher, disk juice; in gray					1,800.00-2,000.00
in red					320.00-345.00
in yellow					38.00-42.00
in Harlequin yellow					50.00-60.00
Pitcher, disk water	125.00-145.00	90.00-105.00	200.00-225.00	900.00-950.00	
Pitcher, ice*	120.00-135.00	90.00-110.00			
Pitcher, 2-pt. jug	85.00-100.00	60.00-70.00	115.00-130.00		

	Red/Ivory Cobalt	Yellow, Turq., Lt. Green	Fifties Colors	Medium Green	As Shown/Specified
Plate, cake*	650.00-700.00	570.00-620.00			
Plate, calendar; 1954, 10"					32.00-38.00
1955, 9"					35.00-42.00
1955, 10"					32.00-38.00
Plate, chop; 13"	35.00-45.00	30.00-35.00	75.00-85.00	150.00-175.00	
15"	52.00-62.00	32.00-42.00	90.00-100.00		
Plate, compartment; 10½"	32.00-38.00	30.00-35.00	55.00-65.00		
12"*	45.00-55.00	42.00-52.00			
Plate, deep	42.00-48.00	32.00-38.00	45.00-50.00	85.00-110.00	
Plate, 6"	5.00-7.00	4.00-5.00	7.00-9.00	14.00-18.00	
Plate, 7"	8.00-10.00	7.00-9.00	10.00-13.00	25.00-30.00	
Plate, 9"	14.00-18.00	9.00-12.00	18.00-22.00	38.00-42.00	
Plate, 10"	35.00-40.00	25.00-30.00	40.00-50.00	85.00-100.00	
Platter	38.00-44.00	25.00-32.00	45.00-55.00	110.00-120.00	
Salt & pepper shakers, pr.	24.00-28.00	15.00-20.00	35.00-40.00	110.00-115.00	
Sauce boat	50.00-60.00	35.00-40.00	60.00-70.00	115.00-130.00	
Saucer	4.00-5.00	3.00-4.00	5.00-6.00	8.00-10.00	
Saucer, demitasse	16.00-20.00	12.00-16.00	75.00-85.00		
Sugar bowl with lid	42.00-52.00	35.00-40.00	60.00-65.00	115.00-130.00	
Sugar bowl, individual					
in turquoise					285.00-310.00
in yellow					85.00-95.00
Syrup*	285.00-310.00	235.00-260.00			
Teacup	28.00-32.00	20.00-25.00	30.00-35.00	45.00-55.00	
Teapot, large*	170.00-190.00	135.00-150.00			
Teapot, medium	150.00-165.00	125.00-140.00	235.00-260.00	575.00-625.00	
Tom and Jerry bowl in ivory with gold letters					225.00-250.00
Tom and Jerry mug in ivory with gold letters					55.00-65.00
Tom and Jerry bowl, not on Fiesta mold (not shown)					50.00-60.00
Tom and Jerry mug, not on Fiesta mold (not shown)					22.00-25.00
Tray, figure-8; in cobalt					65.00-75.00
in turquoise or yellow					210.00-230.00
Tray, relish*					
Center insert	40.00-50.00	32.00-38.00			
Side insert	35.00-40.00	30.00-35.00			
Relish base	70.00-80.00	50.00-60.00			
Tray, relish; gold decorated					190.00-215.00
Tray, utility*	32.00-38.00	30.00-35.00			
Tumbler, juice	35.00-40.00	30.00-35.00			
in rose					45.00-55.00
in chartreuse, Harlequin yellow, or dark green					325.00-375.00
Tumbler, water*	55.00-65.00	45.00-55.00			
Vase, bud*	70.00-80.00	52.00-62.00			
Vase, 8"*	480.00-520.00	400.00-450.00			
Vase, 10"*	630.00-680.00	560.00-610.00			
Vase, 12"*	850.00-900.00	735.00-785.00			

Some feel color is not significant in evaluating the large vases.

Fiesta Ironstone
See Plate 44.
Use the high side of the range to evaluate red Ironstone.

Ashtray, rare	15.00-20.00	Platter, 13"	15.00-18.00
Coffee mug	18.00-22.00	Salad bowl, 10"	38.00-42.00
Coffee server	58.00-68.00	Salt & pepper shakers, pr.	8.00-12.00
Covered casserole	48.00-52.00	Sauce boat	22.00-26.00
Creamer	5.00-7.00	Sauce boat stand	30.00-34.00
Egg cup	6.00-8.00	Sauce boat stand, in red	90.00-110.00
Fruit, small	5.00-6.00	Saucer	1.50-2.00
Marmalade	42.00-48.00	Soup/cereal	5.00-8.00
Nappy, large	15.00-20.00	Soup plate	9.00-12.00
Pitcher, disk water	45.00-55.00	Sugar bowl with lid	9.00-12.00
Plate, 7"	3.00-4.00	Teacup	4.00-5.00
Plate, 10"	6.00-8.00	Teapot, medium	45.00-55.00

Fiesta Kitchen Kraft

See Plates 45 through 57.
Use the high side of the range to evaluate red and cobalt.
Note: See Rhythm section for information concerning gray mixing bowls

Bowl, mixing; 6"..55.00-65.00	Metal frame for platter 22.00-26.00
Bowl, mixing; 8"..72.00-82.00	Pie plate, 9"..40.00-45.00
Bowl, mixing; 10"..85.00-95.00	with advertising in gold 55.00-65.00
Cake plate 48.00-52.00	Pie plate, 10"..40.00-45.00
Cake server 100.00-120.00	in spruce green 250.00-270.00
Casserole, individual 135.00-145.00	Platter 68.00-78.00
Casserole, 7½" 75.00-85.00	Platter in spruce green..............................275.00-300.00
Casserole, 8½" 90.00-100.00	Salt & pepper shakers, pr. 85.00-95.00
Covered jar, large 250.00-275.00	Spoon..95.00-110.00
Covered jar, medium 220.00-240.00	Stacking refrigerator lid 58.00-68.00
Covered jar, small..225.00-250.00	in ivory..160.00-180.00
Covered jug 200.00-220.00	Stacking refrigerator unit 40.00-45.00
Fork..90.00-100.00	in ivory..160.00-180.00

Fiesta Casuals

See Plates 58 and 59.

Yellow Carnation is reported to be harder to find than Daisy, and some collectors feel it should be worth 25% more than suggested values.

Plate, 7"..10.00-12.00	Platter, oval..30.00-36.00
Plate, 10"...12.00-15.00	Saucer 5.00-6.00

Fiesta with Stripes and/or Decals

See Plates 60 through 70.

Of the people we polled on our price survey, the general feeling is that the striped or floral decaled dinnerware should be evaluated at about 30% to 40% more than the prices given for red, ivory, and cobalt Fiesta.

All of the following are Fiesta with the turkey decal:

Plate, 9½"...90.00-105.00
Plate, cake; KK...180.00-200.00
Plate, chop; 13"...110.00-135.00
Plate, chop; 15"...165.00-190.00

Harlequin

See Plates 79 through 96.

Demand has altered the pricing structure for Harlequin. Use the higher side of the high range of values for these colors: maroon, gray, and spruce green. Medium green Harlequin is even more scarce than medium green Fiesta; double the high side of the range for all but the flat pieces and small bowls. Colors represented by the lower end of the high range are chartreuse, dark green, rose, red, light green, and mauve blue. Colors that fall into the low range of values are turquoise and yellow. Those items marked with an asterisk are rare or non-existent in light green; no market value has been established for them.

	Low Range	High Range	As Specified
Ashtray, basketweave	28.00-32.00	45.00-50.00	
Ashtray, regular*	32.00-36.00	45.00-50.00	
Ashtray, saucer*	38.00-42.00	48.00-52.00	
Ashtray, saucer, in ivory			75.00-85.00
Bowl, cream soup	16.00-20.00	22.00-26.00	
Bowl, fruit; 5½"	5.00-7.00	8.00-10.00	
Bowl, individual salad	18.00-22.00	32.00-36.00	
Bowl, mixing; Kitchen Kraft, 6" red or green			70.00-80.00

	Low Range	High Range	As Specified
Bowl, mixing; Kitchen Kraft, 8"			
mauve blue			90.00-110.00
Bowl, mixing; Kitchen Kraft, 10"			
yellow			90.00-110.00
Bowl, nappy, 9"	18.00-22.00	30.00-35.00	
Bowl, oval baker	18.00-22.00	28.00-32.00	
Bowl, 36s	18.00-23.00	30.00-34.00	
in spruce green, maroon, or medium green			55.00-65.00
Bowl, 36s oatmeal	10.00-14.00	18.00-22.00	
Butter dish, ½-lb.	85.00-95.00	90.00-115.00	
Candle holders, pr.*	190.00-210.00	225.00-250.00	
Casserole	78.00-88.00	125.00-140.00	
in medium green			350.00-375.00
Creamer, high-lip; any color			80.00-100.00
Creamer, individual*	15.00-18.00	22.00-28.00	
Creamer, novelty	18.00-22.00	28.00-32.00	
Creamer, regular	8.00-11.00	12.00-16.00	
Cup, demitasse	30.00-38.00	85.00-100.00	
in medium green			150.00-170.00
Cup, large (Epicure body), any color			120.00-145.00
Egg cup, double	12.00-16.00	20.00-24.00	
Egg cup, single*	18.00-22.00	25.00-30.00	
Marmalade, any color*			140.00-165.00
Nut dish, basketweave*	7.00-10.00	10.00-14.00	
Perfume bottle, any color			80.00-100.00
Pitcher, service water	55.00-65.00	75.00-85.00	
Pitcher, 22-oz. jug	30.00-35.00	50.00-60.00	
in medium green			150.00-165.00
Plate, deep	15.00-18.00	20.00-25.00	
in medium green			48.00-58.00
Plate, 6"	3.00-4.00	4.00-5.50	
Plate, 7"	4.00-5.50	6.00-8.00	
Plate, 9"	7.00-9.00	12.00-14.00	
Plate, 10"	15.00-18.00	25.00-30.00	
Platter, 11"	12.00-15.00	18.00-22.00	
Platter, 13"	15.00-20.00	24.00-28.00	
Relish tray, mixed colors*			260.00-280.00
Salt & pepper shakers, pr.	10.00-14.00	15.00-20.00	
Sauce boat	18.00-22.00	24.00-28.00	
Saucer	1.00-2.00	3.00-4.00	
Saucer, demitasse	9.00-12.00	15.00-20.00	
Sugar bowl with lid	12.00-15.00	24.00-28.00	
Syrup, any color*			215.00-235.00
Teacup	7.00-8.50	9.00-11.00	
Teapot	62.00-72.00	110.00-120.00	
Tumbler	35.00-40.00	45.00-50.00	
Tumbler with car decal			45.00-55.00

Harlequin Animals

See Plates 97 through 100.

Any animal in a standard color.............100.00-125.00
Any animal in a non-standard color.....195.00-215.00

Mavericks, near to full-size with gold..........35.00-45.00
smaller, of porcelain-type material........20.00-24.00

Riviera and Ivory Century

See Plates 101 through 117

Batter set, standard colors.................225.00-240.00
with decals...................140.00-155.00
in red, no established value
Bowl, baker, 9".............................16.00-20.00
Bowl, oatmeal; 6".........................28.00-32.00

Bowl, cream soup; with liner in ivory..........60.00-70.00
Liner only.................................20.00-25.00
Bowl, fruit; 5½"................................7.00-10.00
Bowl, nappy, 7¼".............................18.00-22.00
Bowl, utility; ivory.............................44.00-48.00

Butter dish, ½-lb.	85.00-115.00	Plate 10"	38.00-42.00
(See Harlequin listing for price breakdown by color.)		Platter 11½"	15.00-18.00
Butter dish, ¼-lb.	90.00-110.00	Platter, 11¼", closed handles	18.00-20.00
in turquoise	200.00-220.00	Platter, 12", in cobalt	54.00-58.00
in cobalt	190.00-215.00	Platter, 15"	40.00-50.00
Casserole	85.00-95.00	Salt & pepper shakers, pr.	14.00-18.00
Creamer	8.00-11.00	Sauce boat	18.00-22.00
Cup & saucer, demi; ivory	50.00-55.00	Saucer	2.50-3.50
Jug, covered	90.00-115.00	Sugar bowl with lid	14.00-17.50
Jug, open, 4½", ivory	80.00-90.00	Syrup with lid	100.00-125.00
Pitcher, juice; mauve bl.	165.00-185.00	Teacup	7.00-10.00
Pitcher, juice; yellow	90.00-100.00	Teapot	90.00-110.00
Plate, deep	15.00-20.00	Tidbit, 2-tier, in ivory	65.00-75.00
Plate, 6"	6.00-8.00	Tumbler, handled	52.00-58.00
Plate, 7"	8.00-10.00	in ivory	100.00-125.00
in cobalt	25.00-30.00	(These have also been reported in spruce.)	
Plate, 9"	12.00-15.00	Tumbler, juice	40.00-45.00

Amberstone

See Plates 118 through 122.
Items marked with an asterisk (*) are decorated with the black Amberstone pattern.

Ashtray, rare	20.00-25.00	Pie plate *	30.00-35.00
Bowl, jumbo salad	30.00-40.00	Pitcher, disk water	50.00-55.00
Bowl, soup/cereal	5.00-8.00	Plate, bread & butter *	2.50-3.50
Bowl, vegetable	12.00-15.00	Plate, salad *	3.50-4.50
Butter dish *	38.00-42.00	Plate, 10" *	6.00-8.00
Casserole	45.00-50.00	Platter, oval *	12.00-15.00
Coffee server	50.00-55.00	Platter, round serving *	15.00-18.00
Covered jam jar	40.00-45.00	Relish tray, center handle*	22.00-28.00
Covered mustard	50.00-55.00	Salt & pepper shakers, pr.	11.00-13.00
Creamer	6.50-7.50	Sauce boat	16.00-22.00
Cup & saucer *	6.00-8.00	Sauce boat stand	16.00-22.00
Deep soup, 8" *	10.00-12.00	Sugar bowl with lid	7.00-8.50
Dessert dish	5.00-7.00	Tea server	40.00-50.00
Jumbo mug, rare	18.00-22.00		

Carnival

See Plates 123 and 124.

Use the low range of values for these colors: gray, light green, yellow, and dark green. The high side represents values for cobalt, red, ivory, and turquoise.

Fruit, small	5.00-7.00	Plate, 6½"	2.00-3.00
Oatmeal 35s	4.00-6.00	Saucer	1.00-2.00
		Teacup	4.00-6.00

Casualstone

See Plate 125.
Items marked with an asterisk (*) are decorated with the gold Casualstone pattern.

Ashtray, rare	12.00-15.00	Dessert	4.50-5.50
Bowl, jumbo salad; 10"	35.00-38.00	Jumbo mug	12.00-18.00
Bowl, round vegetable	12.00-15.00	Marmalade	40.00-45.00
Bowl, soup/cereal	4.00-6.00	Pie plate *	24.00-28.00
Butter dish, stick*	32.00-38.00	Pitcher, disk type	40.00-45.00
Casserole	40.00-45.00	Plate, bread & butter*	2.50-3.50
Coffee server	40.00-55.00	Plate, dinner*	6.00-8.00
Creamer	4.00-5.00	Plate, salad*	3.50-4.50
Cup & saucer*	6.00-8.00	Platter, oval, 13"*	12.00-15.00
Deep plate*	7.00-8.50	Platter, round*	12.00-15.00

Relish tray* 15.00-18.00	Sugar bowl with lid.........................7.00-8.50
Salt & pepper shakers, pr. 7.00-8.50	Tea server 25.00-30.00
Sauce boat 13.00-17.00	

Epicure

Several people who helped us on our survey reported noticing that Epicure prices are on the rise. Its clean, streamlined styling appeals to the growing number of collectors who are gravitating toward dinnerware with that '50s look.'

See Plates 126 through 127

Bowl, cereal/soup 20.00-25.00	Pickle (small oval platter)............30.00-35.00
Bowl, covered vegetable.............58.00-68.00	Plate, 6½" 6.00-8.00
Bowl, fruit.....................................15.00-20.00	Plate, 8" 14.00-18.00
Bowl, nappy, 8¾" 25.00-30.00	Plate, 10" 18.00-22.00
Casserole, individual 62.00-72.00	Platter, large 22.00-28.00
Coffeepot, 10" 100.00-125.00	Salt & pepper shakers, pr. 16.00-22.00
Creamer..15.00-18.00	Sugar bowl with lid........................20.00-26.00
Gravy bowl 30.00-35.00	Teacup and saucer...........................18.00-22.00
Ladle, 5½"......................................38.00-42.00	2-tier tidbit 45.00-55.00
Nut dish, 4".....................................25.00-30.00	

Jubilee
See Plates 128 through 131.

Bowl, cereal/soup 6.00-8.00	Fiesta juice tumbler 85.00-95.00
Bowl, fruit 4.00-5.00	Plate, 6" 1.50-2.50
Bowl, mixing; KK, 6" 75.00-90.00	Plate, 7" 3.00-4.50
Bowl, mixing; KK, 8" 85.00-100.00	Plate, 9" 5.00-7.00
Bowl, mixing; KK, 10" 100.00-125.00	Plate, 10" 8.00-10.00
Bowl, nappy, 8½" 7.00-9.00	Plate, calendar; cream, 1953.........20.00-25.00
Casserole..25.00-32.00	Plate, chop 12.00-16.00
Coffeepot..30.00-35.00	Platter, 11" 8.00-10.00
Creamer..5.00-6.50	Platter, 13" 9.00-12.00
Cup & saucer....................................4.00-6.50	Salt & pepper shakers, pr 6.00-9.00
Cup & saucer, AD.........................12.00-15.00	Sauce boat 9.00-12.00
Egg cup 7.00-11.00	Sugar bowl with lid........................7.00-10.00
Fiesta juice pitcher 160.00-180.00	Teapot 32.00-40.00

Pastel Nautilus
See Plates 132 through 134.

Bowl, cream soup 9.00-11.00	Egg cup, double.............................12.00-15.00
Bowl, flat soup (deep plate) 7.00-10.00	Gravy boat.......................................12.00-15.00
Bowl, footed oatmeal; 6".............6.00-8.50	Plate, 6" 2.50-3.50
Bowl, fruit; 5"..................................5.00-6.50	Plate, 7" 4.00-5.50
Bowl, tab-handled soup/cereal...............8.00-10.00	Plate, 8" 5.00-6.50
Bowl, oval vegetable 9.00-12.00	Plate, 9" 6.00-8.00
Bowl, round nappy.........................9.00-12.00	Plate, 10" 9.00-12.00
Casserole with lid 38.00-42.00	Platter, 13".......................................12.00-15.00
Creamer..7.00-8.50	Platter, 11"...9.00-12.00
Cup & saucer..................................10.00-12.00	Platter/gravy boat liner, 9".............9.00-12.00
Cup & saucer, AD..........................15.00-18.00	Sugar bowl with lid........................10.00-14.00

Rhythm
See Plates 135 through 141.

Do the 6" and 8" gray mixing bowls really exist? And is the 10" actually worth $200.00 – 250.00 as suggested on our survey? If so, why?

Bowl, ftd cereal/chowder 9.00-12.00	Creamer, 2¾".....................................6.00-8.00
in brown or black..............15.00-20.00	Cup & saucer......................................8.00-10.00
Bowl, fruit; 5½".................................5.00-6.50	Plate, calendar................................9.00-12.00
Bowl, nappy 8.00-12.00	Plate, snack.....................................20.00-25.00
Bowl, mixing; KK, 6" (except gray).....65.00-75.00	Plate, 6" 5.00-6.00
Bowl, mixing; KK, 8" (except gray)......85.00-95.00	Plate, 7" 6.00-7.50
Bowl, mixing; KK, 10" (except gray)...95.00-110.00	Plate, 8", very rare.........................12.00-15.00
Bowl, soup 8.00-10.00	Plate, 9" 7.00-9.00
Casserole, lid only 40.00-50.00	Plate, 10" 10.00-12.00
(bottom is nappy)	

Platter, 11½"	12.00-14.00	Spoon rest, colors other than green	160.00 180.00
Platter, 13½"	14.00-16.00	Spoon rest, in green	220.00-245.00
Salt & pepper shakers, pr	9.00-11.00	Sugar bowl with lid	12.00-15.00
Sauce boat	11.00-14.00	Teapot	38.00-45.00
Sauce boat, in cobalt	16.00-20.00	3-tier tidbit	32.00-38.00
Sauce boat stand	10.00-14.00		

Serenade

See Plates 142 through 146

Bowl, fruit	5.00-7.00	Plate, 9"	6.00-8.00
Bowl, lug soup	15.00-20.00	Plate, 10"	9.00-12.00
Bowl, nappy, 9"	10.00-15.00	Plate, chop	14.00-17.00
Casserole	55.00-65.00	Plate, deep	15.00-18.00
Casserole base, Kitchen Kraft	20.00-25.00	Platter, 12½"	10.00-14.00
Matching lid	40.00-45.00	Salt & pepper shakers, pr	10.00-13.00
Complete	60.00-70.00	Sauce boat	12.00-15.00
Creamer	7.00-9.00	Sugar bowl with lid	9.00-12.00
Pickle dish	9.00-12.00	Teacup & saucer	8.00-10.00
Plate, 6"	2.50-4.00	Teapot	50.00-65.00
Plate, 7"	3.50-5.00		

Tango

See Plate 147.
Use the high side of the range to evaluate red items.

Bowl, fruit; 5¾"	5.00-6.50	Plate, 7"	3.00-4.50
Bowl, nappy, 8¾"	9.00-12.00	Plate, 9"	6.00-8.00
Bowl, oval baker, 9"	9.00-12.00	Plate, 10"	9.00-11.00
Casserole	40.00-50.00	Plate, deep	8.00-11.00
Creamer	6.00-8.00	Platter, 11¾"	9.00-12.00
Cup & saucer	7.00-9.00	Salt & pepper shakers, pr	10.00-12.00
Plate, 6"	2.50-4.00	Sugar bowl with lid	8.00-10.00

Wells Art Glaze

See Plates 148 through 152

Batter set, 3-pc	150.00-165.00	Pickle dish with handles	15.00-18.00
Bowl, cream soup	18.00-22.00	Plate, 6"	4.00-6.00
Bowl, fruit; 5"	8.00-10.00	Plate, 7"	7.00-9.00
Bowl, nappy, 8"	15.00-18.00	Plate, 9"	9.00-12.00
Bowl, oatmeal 36s	15.00-18.00	Plate, 10"	15.00-18.00
Bowl, oval baker, 9"	15.00-18.00	Plate, chop; with handles	15.00-18.00
Casserole	45.00-55.00	Plate, deep	12.00-16.00
Coffeepot, individual	85.00-95.00	Plate, square, 6"	9.00-12.00
Covered jug, 9"	85.00-95.00	Platter, oval, 11½"	15.00-20.00
Covered jug, with decals	45.00-50.00	Platter, oval, 13½"	18.00-22.00
Covered muffin	42.00-48.00	Platter, oval, 15½"	22.00-28.00
Cream soup stand	9.00-12.00	Sauce boat	15.00-20.00
Creamer	15.00-18.00	Sauce boat, fast-stand	20.00-24.00
Cup, bouillon; with handles	15.00-18.00	Sauce boat, liner, handles	12.00-15.00
Cup, coffee; 4¾"	12.00-14.00	Sugar bowl, individual, open	9.00-12.00
Cup & saucer	12.00-16.00	Sugar bowl with lid	12.00-15.00
Cup & saucer, AD	20.00-24.00	Syrup	85.00-95.00
Egg cup, double	15.00-18.00	Syrup, with decals	38.00-42.00
Nut dish/butter pat	8.00-10.00	Teapot	60.00-65.00

Orange Tree Bowls

See Plate 153.

Set of five 180.00-210.00

Mexican Decaled Lines

Conchita, Hacienda, Mexicana, and Max-i-cana

See Plates 155 through 165; 172 through 176.

To simplify the problem of evaluating these lines, we have compiled a general listing that basically will apply to the first three patterns mentioned above (on Century shapes) and Max-i-cana on yellowstone. Our survey showed very little difference in their prices; and the minor variations we did see were not suggestive of a trend, they were simply a matter of personal preference. While some priced Mexicana higher, citing more collector activity in lines more readily available, others felt that because Conchita is harder to find, it should be worth more. Various factors are involved. There are areas of the country where interest in this type of dinnerware is much higher than in other areas. And there seem to be two types of collectors: one who concentrates his interests almost exclusively on the Mexican lines and so is willing to pay more to add to his collection, and one whose interests in Homer Laughlin pottery are a little more diversified. We've done our best to arrive at what appears to be an average. Stressing again that our prices are to be used only as a guide, you may have to make some minor adjustments to reflect market activity in your area. Not all of these items have been found in every pattern. Letter codes have been used to indicate pieces that so far are known to exist in only the coded patterns: H – Hacienda; Me – Mexicana; Ma – Max-i-cana.

Remember that prices given below are for pieces with mint decals. Items with worn or scratched decals are worth no more than chipped ones.

Bell (H) 70.00-85.00	Plate, 9½" (10") 35.00-40.00
Bowl, cream soup; rare (H, Ma) 50.00-60.00	Plate, deep, 8" 18.00-22.00
Bowl, deep, 2½" x 5" (Me) 35.00-40.00	Platter, 10" 15.00-30.00
Bowl, fruit; 5" 9.00-12.00	Platter, oval well, 11½" 28.00-32.00
Bowl, lug soup; 4½" (Ma, Me) 30.00-35.00	Platter, square well, 11½" 28.00-32.00
Bowl, oatmeal; 6" 22.00-25.00	Platter, oval well, 13½" 40.00-45.00
Bowl, vegetable; 8½" 22.00-25.00	Platter, square well, 13½" 40.00-45.00
Bowl, vegetable; 9½" 25.00-28.00	Platter, square well, 15" 30.00-40.00
Butter dish, ½-lb. (H, Ma) 100.00-125.00	Sauce boat 28.00-32.00
round (H) 165.00-190.00	Sauce boat liner (Me, Ma) 25.00-30.00
Casserole 100.00-125.00	Sugar bowl with lid 22.00-28.00
Creamer 15.00-18.00	Sugar, lg. (Ma) 25.00-30.00
Creamer, lg. (Ma) 20.00-25.00	Syrup jug, covered, Century (H, Me) *300.00-400.00
Cup & saucer 15.00-18.00	Tall covered jug, Century (H, Me) *350.00-450.00
Egg cup, torpedo shape (Me, Ma) 30.00-35.00	Teapot, rare (H, Me) 125.00-130.00
Egg cup, rolled edge (Me, Ma) 30.00-40.00	Tumbler, fired-on design, 6-oz. 9.00-12.00
Plate, 6" 4.00-6.00	Tumbler, fired-on design, 8-oz. 12.00-16.00
Plate, 7" 9.00-12.00	Tumbler, fired-on design, 10-oz. 15.00-18.00
Plate, 9" 15.00-20.00	*Open jugs are worth ½ as much as those w/lids.

Kitchen Kraft Conchita and Mexicana

See Plates 155, 157, 158 and 176.

Again we found that some collectors value Conchita more highly than Mexicana. Depending upon whom you deal with, you may have to pay more for it, though most of our correspondents felt that intrinsically their values should be interchangeable.

Batter jug with lid 138.00-152.00	Covered jar, large 120.00-135.00
open 100.00-115.00	Covered jar, medium 90.00-110.00
Bowl, mixing; 6" 24.00-28.00	Covered jar, small...........................90.00-110.00
Bowl, mixing; 8" 28.00-32.00	Fork...50.00-58.00
Bowl, mixing; 10" 35.00-40.00	Pie plate 28.00-32.00
Cake plate, 10½" 28.00-32.00	Refrigerator stack unit 40.00-45.00
Cake server 50.00-60.00	lid 45.00-50.00
Casserole, individual 80.00-90.00	Salt & pepper shakers, pr 45.00-50.00
Casserole, 7½" 68.00-78.00	Spoon...52.00-58.00
Casserole, 8½" 65.00-75.00	Underplate, 9" 32.00-38.00
Oven Serve, Handy Andy 50.00-58.00	Underplate, 6" (rare) 30.00-40.00
Metal base 14.00-18.00	

Max-i-cana Fiesta

Cup & saucer	35.00-40.00	Plate, 6"	12.00-15.00
Fruit, 5½"	28.00-32.00	Plate, 10"	35.00-40.00
Nappy, 8½"	40.00-45.00	Platter	40.00-50.00

Miscellaneous Mexican Lines

After carefully studying the results of our survey, we found very little difference between the average of the values suggested above for 'Conchita, Hacienda, Mexicana, and Max-i-cana on yellowstone' and the values offered for the less-familiar lines such as Mexicali Virginia Rose. So in order to simplify using this section of the price guide, we suggest that for any Mexican decal on shapes such as Swing, Nautilus, Virginia Rose, and Harlequin use 'Conchita, Hacienda, Mexicana, and Max-i-cana on yellowstone' values, placing the top of the value range for the miscellaneous lines at its low end (for the flat pieces) to about the middle range (for the molded hollowware). The harder-to-find items such as the butter dish, egg cup, and casserole, for instance, will bring just as much in one Mexican decaled line as another.

Go-Alongs

Plate 180: Pitcher with fired-on Mexican figures	32.00-38.00
Tumbler	8.00-12.00
Plate 181: Coaster set	12.00-15.00
Napkin ring, ea.	4.00-5.00
Placecard holder, ea.	4.00-5.00
Tumbler with raffia wrap & enameled cactus	8.00-12.00
Plate 182: Metal frame for Fiesta jam set (cream soup)	60.00-70.00
Metal frame for Fiesta marmalade	70.00-80.00
Metal frame for Fiesta chop plate	35.00-42.00
Plate 183: Metal frame for Fiesta salad service set	80.00-90.00
Not shown:	
Metal frame for Fiesta mustard & marmalade	65.00-75.00
Metal frame for Fiesta cake plate	35.00-40.00
Metal revolving base for Fiesta relish tray	28.00-32.00
Shown in artist's rendering:	
Metal frame for Fiesta promotional casserole	30.00-35.00
Metal frame for Fiesta condiment set (mustard & shakers)	65.00-75.00
Metal frame for Fiesta double tidbit set with folding stand	80.00-90.00
Plate 184: Fiesta 3-tier tidbit tray (in mixed colors)	90.00-100.00
(Add 10% for each plate in red, ivory, or cobalt — 20% for each plate in the fifties colors)	
Plate 185: Metal holder for Harlequin tumbler	18.00-22.00
Plate 186: Wireware donkey holder for Harlequin shakers	20.00-25.00
Plate 187: Harlequin nut dish	40.00-50.00
Plate 188: Century 2-tier tidbit tray in ivory	60.00-70.00
Plate 189: Century nut dish in ivory	50.00-60.00
Plate 190: Hankscraft egg cup	6.00-8.00
Hankscraft egg poacher with glass insert	45.00-50.00
Plate 191: Metal popcorn set, 5-pc., excellent paint	75.00-85.00
Plate 192: Frame for Fiesta ice-lip pitcher & tumblers (watch for repros)	60.00-70.00
Plate 193: Metal 3-part tidbit set, mint condition paint	60.00-70.00
Plate 194: Metal handle for Fiesta mixing-bowl ice bucket	40.00-45.00
Plate 195: Wooden tray/metal base for Fiesta chop plate	50.00-65.00
Plate 196: Fiestawood salad bowl	75.00-90.00
Plate 197: Insert for Fiestawood tray	15.00-18.00
Plate 198: Metal holder for Fiesta nappy	18.00-22.00
Metal dripolator insert for Fiesta teapot	10.00-16.00
Metal frame for Fiesta jam set	45.00-50.00
Wireware holder for Fiesta juice set	50.00-60.00
Sta-Bright Flatware, 3-pc. setting	8.00-10.00
Fiestawood tray with glass insert	90.00-100.00
Not shown:	
Metal holder for Kitchen Kraft platter	20.00-24.00
Metal holder for Kitchen Kraft pie plate	15.00-20.00
Metal holder for Kitchen Kraft casserole	15.00-20.00

Plate 199: Fiestawood salad bowl...75.00-85.00
Plate 200: Fiestawood hors d'oeuvres tray 70.00-80.00
Plate 201: Cabinet, no established value.
Plate 202: Fiestawood hors d'oeuvres tray 70.00-80.00
Plate 203: Sheet of decals 50.00-60.00
Plate 204: Ash stand 80.00-100.00
Plate 205: Metal Kitchenware bread box..50.00-60.00
Plate 206: Metal Kitchenware bread box..50.00-60.00
          Metal Kitchenware garbage can 65.00-80.00
Plate 207: Metal Kitchenware canister set, 4-pc., mint in box 70.00-90.00
          Metal Kitchenware napkin holder 40.00-45.00
Not shown:
          Metal Kitchenware stool 80.00-100.00
          Metal Kitchenware waste can 45.00-50.00
          Metal Kitchenware 3-tier vegetable bin...65.00-75.00
Plate 208: Quick Cut flatware set, mint in box 65.00-75.00
Plate 209: Sta Bright flatware, large boxed set, per item.......................................7.00-8.50
Not shown:
          Luncheon set, tablecloth & 4 napkins
          circa 1930s-'40s, color & design compatible..25.00-30.00

Commercial Adapations and Ephemera

Plates 210: Fiesta price lists, 1930s through 1940s...45.00-55.00
          1940s through 1950s..32.00-38.00
          1950s on 30.00-35.00
Plate 211: Riviera price list 50.00-60.00
Plate 212: Fiesta Kitchen Kraft price list 52.00-58.00
Plate 213: Harlequin price list 50.00-60.00
Not shown:
          Jubilee price list 25.00-35.00
Plate 214: Fiesta store display, complete, NM..800.00-1,000.00
Plate 215: Fiesta carton, small 25.00-30.00
          Fiesta carton, large 30.00-40.00
Plate 216: Fiesta carton for dinnerware set 60.00-80.00
Not shown:
          Fiesta carton for juice set (no dancing girl logo) 25.00-30.00
Plate 217: Fiesta Ensemble display ad 120.00-135.00
Plate 218: National Dairy Council punch-outs, as shown 100.00-125.00
Plate 219: Soup can label 6.00-7.50
Plate 220: Fiesta syrup with Dutchess tea 80.00-90.00
Plate 221: Fiesta egg cup, Lazarus Anniversary..45.00-50.00
Plate 222: Fiesta ash-tray, commemorative or advertising....................................60.00-70.00
Plate 223: Fiesta on Homemaker's Recipe File 12.00-15.00
Plate 224: Riviera on corn package 5.00-8.00
Plate 225: New Fiesta mug, no established value.
Plate 226: Buick Sit n' Sip coasters..22.00-28.00
Plate 227: Fiesta Tom & Jerry mugs in white (or color inside)
          1–color advertising 35.00-40.00
          2–color advertising 40.00-45.00
          3–color advertising 48.00-52.00
          4–color advertising 56.00-62.00
          Fiesta Tom & Jerry mugs in color with advertising.................................60.00-70.00
          Fiesta Tom & Jerry mugs, color inside, no advertising 25.00-30.00
          Matching Sit n' Sip coasters...22.00-28.00
Plate 228: Buick Tom & Jerry mugs..60.00-70.00

The Morgue; Experimentals; Inventions

Because most of the items shown in these chapters are one of a kind or at least extremely rare, market values
have not been established. The maroon mug in Plate 251 is one from a set of fifteen which along with a large bowl
was dipped at the factory as a special gift for a supervisor. The average suggested price on our last mail survey was
$800.00 to $1,000.00, and that estimate remains stable.

Plate 253: Harlequin lamp with fabricated body...250.00-270.00
Plate 254 & 255: Syrup lamp base, undecorated 200.00-220.00

Syrup lamp base, hand painted 210.00-235.00
With original shade, add...30.00-35.00
Plate 256: Fiesta lamp with fabricated body 260.00-280.00

Kitchen Kraft; Oven-Serve

See Plates 257 through 261.

Use the higher side to evaluate the more collectible lines such as Sun Porch, Kitchen Bouquet, etc.

Bowl, mixing; 6"	15.00-20.00	Covered jar, large	90.00-105.00
Bowl, mixing; 8"	18.00-22.00	Covered jug	80.00-90.00
Bowl, mixing; 10"	25.00-30.00	Fork	35.00-40.00
Casserole, individual	50.00-58.00	Pie plate	25.00-30.00
Casserole, 6"	30.00-35.00	Platter	35.00-40.00
Casserole, 8½"	32.00-38.00	Metal base	20.00-24.00
Metal base	15.00-20.00	Salt and pepper shakers, pr.	38.00-42.00
Cake server	35.00-40.00	Spoon	35.00-40.00
Cake plate	28.00-32.00	Stacking refrigerator lid	28.00-32.00
Covered jar, small	60.00-70.00	Stacking refrigerator unit	22.00-28.00
Covered jar, medium	80.00-88.00	Underplate	18.00-22.00

Embossed Line

See Plates 262 through 264.
Add 50% when decals are present.

Batter pitcher	40.00-50.00	Casserole, 6"	10.00-12.00
Bean pot, 4x4½"	10.00-12.00	Casserole, 7½"	20.00-25.00
Bean pot, 4¼x5½"	10.00-12.00	Casserole, 8½"	25.00-30.00
Bowl, 4"	4.00-5.50	Casserole, 10"	32.00-38.00
Bowl, fruit; 5½"	8.00-10.00	Cup, 3¾", rare	15.00-18.00
Bowl, mixing; 6¼"	9.00-12.00	Custard cup, 3½"	4.00-5.00
Bowl, mixing; 7¼"	12.00-15.00	Pie plate, 9"	16.00-20.00
Bowl, mixing; 8½"	16.00-20.00	Plate, 7"	5.00-7.00
Bowl, oval baker, 6½"	7.00-8.50	Plate, 10"	8.00-10.00
Bowl, oval baker, 8½"	10.00-12.00	Platter, deep, oval, 8"	10.00-12.00
Bowl, oval baker, 11"	15.00-20.00	Platter, deep oval, 12"	14.00-16.00
Bowl, ramekin, handled, 4½"	5.00-6.00	Saucer, 5¾"	1.50-2.00
Bowl, tab-handled soup; 7"	9.00-10.00		

Americana

See Plate 265.

Bowl, dessert/fruit	5.00-6.00	Plate, 7"	5.00-7.00
Bowl, coupe soup	8.00-12.00	Plate, 8½"	12.00-15.00
Bowl, cream soup	60.00-75.00	Plate, 10"	20.00-24.00
Bowl, oval vegetable, 8½"	18.00-22.00	Plate, 8" sq.	12.00-15.00
Bowl, round vegetable, 8"	18.00-22.00	Platter, 11"	14.00-18.00
Bowl, round vegetable, 9"	22.00-26.00	Platter, 13"	20.00-24.00
Bowl, lid, 9"	22.00-26.00	Platter, 15"	48.00-52.00
Creamer	12.00-15.00	Platter, round, 13"	22.00-26.00
Cup & saucer	9.00-12.00	Sauce boat	20.00-24.00
Cup & saucer, AD	18.00-22.00	Sauce boat stand	18.00-22.00
Egg cup	12.00-16.00	Sugar bowl with lid	15.00-18.00
Plate, 6"	3.00-4.00	Teapot	70.00-78.00

Decaled Century

See Plates 266 through 269.

Because it is impossible to list every Century-based dinnerware line produced by HLC, we offer these suggestions to help you determine approximately how much you should expect to pay for the following:

1) For place-setting items (plates, cups and saucers, small bowls, etc.) purchased one at a time in a very simple pattern, use Carnival prices.

2) For place-setting items purchased one at a time in a more desirable pattern of Mexicana prices.

3) For larger serving pieces or purchases of larger lots of a very simple pattern, use 50% of Mexicana prices.
4) For larger serving pieces or purchases of larger lots of a more desirable pattern, use 75% of Mexicana prices.

Children's Sets

Plate 270: Ralston bowl...35.00-40.00
Plate 271: Tom & the Butterfly, 3-pc. set 125.00-140.00
Plate 272: Dick Tracy, 3-pc. set 225.00-245.00
    Plate 60.00-70.00
    Soup/cereal 75.00-85.00
    Mug..75.00-85.00
Plate 273: Animal characters on Fiesta shapes, set 475.00-525.00
    On shapes other than Fiesta 125.00-135.00

Dogwood

See Plates 274 and 275.
Values are given for pieces with excellent gold trim.

Bowl, cereal; 6"....................8.00-10.00	Plate, 6" 4.00-5.00
Bowl, fruit; 5¾"......................5.00-6.00	Plate, 7" 8.00-10.00
Bowl, mixing; KK, 6½" 30.00-35.00	Plate, 8", scarce.....................10.00-12.00
Bowl, mixing; KK, 8¾" 30.00-35.00	Plate, 9" 7.00-8.00
Bowl, mixing; KK, 10½" 30.00-35.00	Plate, 10", scarce...................10.00-12.00
Bowl, soup; 8"......................10.00-12.00	Platter, 11¾"..........................18.00-20.00
Bowl, round vegetable, 8¾" 18.00-20.00	Platter, 13½"..........................20.00-25.00
Bowl, oval vegetable, 9½"..........18.00-20.00	Sauce boat.............................18.00-20.00
Creamer.............................10.00-12.00	Sauce boat liner, 8½" 20.00-25.00
Cup & saucer........................9.00-10.00	Sugar bowl with lid.................18.00-20.00
	Teapot 60.00-70.00

Harmony Lines

See Plates 276 through 278.

For Kitchen Kraft items not listed here, use the high side of the range of values suggested for Kitchen Kraft on page 185.

Bowl, cereal/soup 10.00-12.00	Cup & saucer.........................7.00-10.00
Bowl, oval baker, 10"..............15.00-20.00	Fork, KK................................40.00-45.00
Bowl, fruit; 5½"......................5.00-7.00	Pie plate, KK, 10" 25.00-30.00
Bowl, mixing; KK, 10" 28.00-32.00	Plate, 6" 3.00-4.00
Bowl, nappy, 9" 12.00-15.00	Plate, 7" 5.00-8.00
Cake server, KK 40.00-45.00	Plate, 9" 6.00-9.00
Casserole, KK, 8"...................35.00-40.00	Spoon, KK...............................40.00-45.00
Casserole, KK, individual.........40.00-50.00	

Historical American Subjects

See Plate 279.

To evaluate this line, use suggested prices for Americana.

Jade

See Plate 280.

Values for decaled Jade may be computed by using the suggestions under 'Decaled Century.'

Nautilus

See Plate 281.

Values for decaled Nautilus (other than Harmony) may be computed by using the suggestions under 'Decaled Century.'

Priscilla

See Plates 282 and 283.
Values are given for pieces with excellent gold trim.

Bowl, fruit; 5"...............................5.00-6.00	Plate, 8"...8.00-9.00
Bowl, fruit; KK, 9½", scarce.............25.00-30.00	Plate, 9"...8.00-9.00
Bowl, mixing; small, KK, 6"................25.00-30.00	Plate, 10"....................................10.00-12.00
Bowl, mixing; medium, KK, 8"..............25.00-30.00	Platter, 9"...................................15.00-18.00
Bowl, mixing; large, KK, 10"...............25.00-30.00	Platter, 13½"................................20.00-25.00
Bowl, oval vegetable; 9"....................18.00-20.00	Platter, tab-handled,
Bowl, round vegetable, 8" 18.00-20.00	(made by Universal)...............20.00-25.00
Bowl, soup; 8"...............................10.00-12.00	Pitcher, water; KK..........................25.00-30.00
Cake plate, KK, 11".........................15.00-18.00	Pie plate, KK, 9½" 20.00-25.00
Casserole, round, KK, 8½"...............25.00-28.00	Sauce boat...................................18.00-20.00
Coffeepot, KK................................70.00-75.00	Sugar bowl with lid........................18.00-20.00
Creamer.......................................10.00-12.00	Teapot, Republic, hard to find.........65.00-75.00
Cup & saucer..................................9.00-10.00	Teapot, regular.............................65.00-75.00
Plate, 6"...4.00-5.00	Teapot, tall, hard to find
Plate, 7"...6.00-7.00	(made by Universal)...............65.00-75.00

Rhythm

See Plates 284 through 286.

Plate 284: Western Bowl, fruit...............10.00-12.00	Cup & saucer................................12.00-15.00
Bowl, vegetable 15.00-20.00	Plate, 9".......................................12.00-15.00
Plate 285: American Provincial	
Spoon rest.............................80.00-100.00	
Plate 286: Rhythm Rose	
Bowl, mixing; KK, small 12.00-14.00	Pitcher, jug type, KK.....................25.00-35.00
Bowl, mixing; KK, med 15.00-18.00	Plate, 6"...3.00-4.00
Bowl, mixing; KK, large 18.00-22.00	Plate, 9"...6.00-8.00
Cake plate, KK, 10½" 15.00-20.00	Plate, deep, 8"..............................10.00-12.00
Cake server, KK....................25.00-35.00	Platter, 13"...................................12.00-15.00
Casserole, KK, 8½" 30.00-35.00	Sauce boat.....................................9.00-12.00
Cup & saucer, AD...............14.00-16.00	Sugar bowl with lid........................10.00-12.00
Coffeepot, KK 30.00-35.00	Underplate, KK, 6" 8.00-11.00
Creamer.................................6.00-8.00	Underplate, KK, 9" 10.00-13.00
Pie plate, KK, 9½".................14.00-16.00	

Swing

See Plates 287 through 289.

Values for decaled Swing dinnerware lines may be computed by using the suggestions under 'Decaled Century.'

Virginia Rose

See Plates 290 through 293.
Values are given for pieces with excellent gold or silver trim.

Bowl, covered vegetable, 9" 80.00-90.00	Mug, coffee...................................25.00-35.00
Bowl, deep, 5"................................12.00-15.00	Pitcher, milk; 5"............................25.00-30.00
Bowl, fruit; 5½"................................5.00-7.00	Pitcher, water; 7½".......................80.00-100.00
Bowl, mixing; KK, 6".........................30.00-35.00	Plate, 6"...5.00-6.00
Bowl, mixing; KK, 8".........................30.00-35.00	Plate, 7".......................................8.00-10.00
Bowl, mixing; KK, 10".......................30.00-35.00	Plate, 8", scarce...........................12.00-15.00
Bowl, oatmeal; 6" 8.00-10.00	Plate, 9"...7.00-8.00
Bowl, oval vegetable; 8" scarce 20.00-25.00	Plate, 10"....................................10.00-12.00
Bowl, oval vegetable; 9"....................15.00-20.00	Plate, deep; 1" flange.....................15.00-18.00
Bowl, oval vegetable; 10"..................20.00-25.00	Plate, deep; no flange.....................15.00-18.00
Bowl, vegetable; 7½", scarce...............20.00-25.00	Platter/gravy liner, 9"....................20.00-25.00
Bowl, vegetable; 8½" 20.00-25.00	Platter, 10½", scarce......................20.00-25.00
Bowl, vegetable; 9½" 25.00-30.00	Platter, 11½"................................15.00-20.00
Butter dish, ½-lb.............................80.00-100.00	Platter, 13"...................................20.00-25.00

Cake plate, KK 40.00-50.00	Platter, 15½" 30.00-35.00
Cake server, KK 25.00-30.00	Pie plate, KK, 9½" 20.00-25.00
Casserole, KK, Oven Serve:	Pie plate, KK, 12", scarce 25.00-30.00
Round sides, 7½" or 8½", scarce.....30.00-35.00	Tray with handles, 8" 20.00-25.00
Straight sides, scarce.....................40.00-50.00	Salt & pepper shakers:
Creamer...10.00-12.00	Regular, scarce, pr 70.00-75.00
Cup & saucer....................................9.00-10.00	KK, scarce, pr 70.00-75.00
Egg cup, double 35.00-40.00	Sauce boat..20.00-25.00
	Sugar bowl with lid...........................15.00-20.00

Laughlin Art China

Plate 294: Bowl, ruffled, Currant, 2"x10" 125.00-150.00
     Plate, Currant, 9½" 50.00-70.00
     Plate, scalloped, Currant, 10" 60.00-80.00
Plate 295: Humidor, wooden lid, Currant, 5"x 6" 175.00-200.00
     Pitcher, bulbous, Currant, 4½"x 5" 85.00-100.00
     Orange bowl with handles, Currant, 12" 150.00-175.00
     Pitcher, straight sides, Currant, 6½" 110.00-130.00
Plate 296: Bread tray, Fe Dora, Currant, 12½" 75.00-90.00
Plate 297: Chocolate pot, Currant 240.00-275.00
     Chocolate cup & saucer, Currant 80.00-100.00
Plate 298: Vase, Currant, 7" 75.00-100.00
Plate 299: Covered dish, Currant 165.00-190.00
Plate 300: Pitcher, Dutch Jug, Currant, 10" 130.00-150.00
Plate 301: Vase, Currant, 9¾" 125.00-150.00
     Vase, slim form, Currant, 12" 120.00-140.00
     Vase, slim form, Currant, 16" 200.00-225.00
     Chocolate/AD pot, Currant, 10" 175.00-200.00
Plate 302: Vase, Currant, 12½" 170.00-190.00
Plate 303: Vase, with handles, Currant, 14" 275.00-300.00
Plate 304: Chocolate cup & saucer, gold trim, Flow Blue..............................130.00-150.00
Plate 305: Bonbon, gold trim, Flow Blue..130.00-150.00
Plate 306: Sugar basket, Golden Fleece 175.00-200.00
     Sugar basket, Currant 160.00-180.00
Plate 307: Pitcher, milk; White Pets 150.00-175.00
Plate 308: Jardiniere, lady's, gold trim, Flow Blue, 5½"x 8" 250.00-300.00
     Vase, lady & peacock, gold trim, 12" 250.00-300.00
     Mug, monk, stag handle..60.00-75.00
Plate 309: Tankard, American Beauty 250.00-300.00
     Mug, American Beauty..80.00-100.00
Plate 310: Pitcher, milk; plums 95.00-115.00
Plate 311: Tankard, American Floral..250.00-300.00
Plate 312: Stein, football player 240.00-270.00
Plate 314: Stein, advertising..165.00-185.00
Additional Art China, not shown:
     Bowl, 17th-century child in center, gold trim, ruffled, Flow Blue 130.00-150.00
     Bowl, American Beauty, 10" 110.00-125.00
     Cake plate, with handles, Fe Dora, Currant, 10" 90.00-105.00
     Jardiniere, with handles, gold trim, Flow Blue, 10"x14"....................500.00-600.00
     Mug, Jacobean design 60.00-70.00
     Mug, Monk..60.00-70.00
     Tankard, Monk..150.00-175.00
     Stein, White Pets..125.00-150.00
     Vase, with handles, White Pets, 8"..210.00-230.00
     Vase, White Pets, with cats, shape as shown in Plate 303 ....300.00-350.00
     Orange bowl, lady and peacock, shape shown in Plate 295 ....250.00-275.00
     Bowl, lady and peacock, 9" 175.00-200.00
     Mug, lady and peacock design, woman feeding birds 110.00-125.00
     Tankard, Currant..250.00-275.00
     Mug, Currant 60.00-75.00
     Plate, White Pets, child and donkey 110.00-125.00
     Milk pitcher, with plums..125.00-150.00
     Creamer (matches Golden Fleece sugar basket) 85.00-100.00
     Creamer (matches Currant sugar basket) 85.00-100.00
     Plate, Currant, 7" 30.00-40.00
     Rose bowl, Currant, 4"..125.00-150.00

Dreamland and Similar Lines

Plate 314: Stein, Dreamland..120.00-150.00
        Tankard, Dreamland...225.00-250.00
Plate 315: Vase, 3½"..115.00-125.00
Plate 316: Bowl, ruffled, Dreamland, 10"..150.00-175.00
        Jug..150.00-175.00
Plate 317: Orange bowl, Laughlin's Holland* 165.00-190.00
Plate 318: Pitcher, Genesee, ca 1915, 3½"..70.00-90.00
        New Item: Dreamland plate, 10"...150.00-175.00

World's Fair
The American Potter

Plate 319: Cake set, Cronin China Co..60.00-70.00
        Bowl, Paden City Pottery, 10"...60.00-70.00
        Plate, Knowles, 10¾"...60.00-70.00
        Marmalade, complete, Edwin Knowles...60.00-70.00
        Pitcher, Porcelier..85.00-100.00
Plate 320: Plate, Golden Gate Expo, either year..80.00-100.00
        Ash tray, Golden Gate Expo 75.00-85.00
Plate 321: Plate HLC World's Fair 110.00-120.00
Plate 322: Pitcher, George Washington, ivory, 5"..42.00-46.00
        Pitcher, Martha Washington, ivory, 5"...42.00-46.00
        Pitcher, in ivory, 2", either George or Martha 30.00-35.00
        As shown, cobalt, No established value
Plate 323: Bowl, Four Seasons, each 52.00-58.00
Plate 324: Vase, 5" to 8"..80.00-100.00
        Under 5"..50.00-60.00
Plate 325: Plate, Potters; either view
        In turquoise or tan..38.00-42.00
        In ivory or green..48.00-52.00
        Cup & saucer, Zodiac 65.00-75.00
Not shown:
        Salt & pepper shakers, George & Martha Washington 45.00-50.00
        Candle holder 40.00-45.00
        Individual creamer, etched World's Fair.......................................45.00-55.00
        Toothpick holder, George & Martha Washington, ivory 45.00-55.00

Miscellaneous

Plate 324: Sit n' Sip, see Commercial Adaptations for pricing information.
Plate 327: Nude vase...300.00-350.00
        Donkey ashtray..450.00-500.00
Plate 328: Bill Booth football..700.00-850.00

Values For Our Early Editions

The earlier editions of our Fiesta book have themselves become sought-after collectibles. Remember that condition is important, and values are given for copies in very fine condition.

First Edition..100.00-135.00
Second Edition...65.00-75.00
Third Edition..40.00-50.00
Fourth Edition 35.00-45.00
Fifth Edition 20.00-25.00

COLLECTOR BOOKS
Informing Today's Collector

For over two decades we have been keeping collectors informed on trends and values in all fields of antiques and collectibles.

DOLLS, FIGURES & TEDDY BEARS

2382	**Advertising Dolls**, Identification & Values, Robison & Sellers	$9.95
2079	**Barbie** Doll Fashions, Volume I, Eames	$24.95
3957	**Barbie** Exclusives, Rana	$18.95
4557	**Barbie**, The First 30 Years, Deutsch	$24.95
3310	**Black Dolls**, 1820–1991, Perkins	$17.95
3873	**Black Dolls**, Book II, Perkins	$17.95
3810	**Chatty Cathy** Dolls, Lewis	$15.95
2021	Collectible **Action Figures**, 2nd Ed., Manos	$14.95
1529	Collector's Encyclopedia of **Barbie** Dolls, DeWein	$19.95
4506	Collector's Guide to **Dolls in Uniform**, Bourgeois	$18.95
3727	Collector's Guide to **Ideal Dolls**, Izen	$18.95
3728	Collector's Guide to Miniature **Teddy Bears**, Powell	$17.95
3967	Collector's Guide to **Trolls**, Peterson	$19.95
4569	**Howdy Doody**, Collector's Reference and Trivia Guide, Koch	$16.95
1067	**Madame Alexander** Dolls, Smith	$19.95
3971	**Madame Alexander** Dolls Price Guide #20, Smith	$9.95
3733	**Modern Collector's** Dolls, Sixth Series, Smith	$24.95
3991	**Modern Collector's** Dolls, Seventh Series, Smith	$24.95
4571	**Liddle Kiddles,** Identification & Value Guide, Langford	$18.95
3972	Patricia Smith's **Doll Values**, Antique to Modern, 11th Edition	$12.95
3826	Story of **Barbie,** Westenhouser	$19.95
1513	**Teddy Bears & Steiff** Animals, Mandel	$9.95
1817	**Teddy Bears & Steiff** Animals, 2nd Series, Mandel	$19.95
2084	**Teddy Bears, Annalee's & Steiff** Animals, 3rd Series, Mandel	$19.95
1808	Wonder of **Barbie,** Manos	$9.95
1430	World of **Barbie** Dolls, Manos	$9.95

FURNITURE

1457	American **Oak** Furniture, McNerney	$9.95
3716	American **Oak** Furniture, Book II, McNerney	$12.95
1118	Antique **Oak** Furniture, Hill	$7.95
2132	Collector's Encyclopedia of **American** Furniture, Vol. I, Swedberg	$24.95
2271	Collector's Encyclopedia of **American** Furniture, Vol. II, Swedberg	$24.95
3720	Collector's Encyclopedia of **American** Furniture, Vol. III, Swedberg	$24.95
1437	Collector's Guide to **Country** Furniture, Raycraft	$9.95
3878	Collector's Guide to **Oak** Furniture, George	$12.95
1755	Furniture of the **Depression Era,** Swedberg	$19.95
3906	**Heywood-Wakefield** Modern Furniture, Rouland	$18.95
1965	**Pine** Furniture, Our American Heritage, McNerney	$14.95
1885	**Victorian** Furniture, Our American Heritage, McNerney	$9.95
3829	**Victorian** Furniture, Our American Heritage, Book II, McNerney	$9.95
3869	**Victorian** Furniture books, 2 volume set, McNerney	$19.90

JEWELRY, HATPINS, WATCHES & PURSES

1712	Antique & Collector's **Thimbles** & Accessories, Mathis	$19.95
1748	Antique **Purses**, Revised Second Ed., Holiner	$19.95
1278	Art Nouveau & Art Deco **Jewelry**, Baker	$9.95
4558	Christmas Pins, Past and Present, Gallina	$18.95
3875	Collecting Antique **Stickpins**, Kerins	$16.95
3722	Collector's Ency. of **Compacts, Carryalls & Face Powder Boxes**, Mueller	$24.95
3992	Complete Price Guide to **Watches**, #15, Shugart	$21.95
1716	Fifty Years of Collectible **Fashion Jewelry**, 1925-1975, Baker	$19.95
1424	**Hatpins** & Hatpin Holders, Baker	$9.95
4570	Ladies' **Compacts**, Gerson	$24.95
1181	100 Years of Collectible **Jewelry**, 1850-1950, Baker	$9.95
2348	20th Century Fashionable Plastic **Jewelry**, Baker	$19.95
3830	Vintage **Vanity Bags & Purses**, Gerson	$24.95

TOYS, MARBLES & CHRISTMAS COLLECTIBLES

3427	**Advertising Character** Collectibles, Dotz	$17.95
2333	Antique & Collector's **Marbles**, 3rd Ed., Grist	$9.95
3827	Antique & Collector's **Toys**, 1870–1950, Longest	$24.95
3956	Baby Boomer **Games,** Identification & Value Guide, Polizzi	$24.95
3717	**Christmas** Collectibles, 2nd Edition, Whitmyer	$24.95
1752	**Christmas** Ornaments, Lights & Decorations, Johnson	$19.95
3874	Collectible Coca-Cola Toy **Trucks,** deCourtivron	$24.95
2338	Collector's Encyclopedia of **Disneyana,** Longest, Stern	$24.95
2151	Collector's Guide to **Tootsietoys**, 2nd Ed., Richter	$16.95
3436	Grist's Big Book of **Marbles**	$19.95
3970	Grist's Machine-Made & Contemporary **Marbles,** 2nd Ed.	$9.95
3732	**Matchbox®** Toys, 1948 to 1993, Johnson	$18.95
3823	**Mego** Toys, An Illustrated Value Guide, Chrouch	15.95
1540	**Modern Toys** 1930–1980, Baker	$19.95
3888	**Motorcycle** Toys, Antique & Contemporary, Gentry/Downs	$18.95
3891	Schroeder's Collectible **Toys,** Antique to Modern Price Guide, 2nd Ed.	$17.95
1886	Stern's Guide to **Disney** Collectibles	$14.95
2139	Stern's Guide to **Disney** Collectibles, 2nd Series	$14.95
3975	Stern's Guide to **Disney** Collectibles, 3rd Series	$18.95
2028	**Toys**, Antique & Collectible, Longest	$14.95
3975	**Zany Characters** of the Ad World, Lamphier	$16.95

INDIANS, GUNS, KNIVES, TOOLS, PRIMITIVES

1868	Antique **Tools,** Our American Heritage, McNerney	$9.95
2015	Archaic **Indian** Points & Knives, Edler	$14.95
1426	**Arrowheads** & Projectile Points, Hothem	$7.95
2279	**Indian** Artifacts of the Midwest, Hothem	$14.95
3885	**Indian** Artifacts of the Midwest, Book II, Hothem	$16.95
1964	**Indian** Axes & Related Stone Artifacts, Hothem	$14.95
2023	**Keen Kutter** Collectibles, Heuring	$14.95
3887	Modern **Guns,** Identification & Values, 10th Ed., Quertermous	$12.95
4505	Standard Guide to **Razors**, Ritchie & Stewart	$9.95
3325	Standard **Knife** Collector's Guide, 2nd Ed., Ritchie & Stewart	$12.95

PAPER COLLECTIBLES & BOOKS

1441	Collector's Guide to **Post Cards**, Wood	$9.95
2081	Guide to Collecting **Cookbooks**, Allen	$14.95
3969	Huxford's **Old Book** Value Guide, 7th Ed.	$19.95
3821	Huxford's **Paperback** Value Guide	$19.95
2080	Price Guide to **Cookbooks & Recipe Leaflets**, Dickinson	$9.95
2346	**Sheet Music** Reference & Price Guide, 2nd Ed., Pafik & Guiheen	$18.95

GLASSWARE

1006	**Cambridge Glass** Reprint 1930–1934	$14.95
1007	**Cambridge Glass** Reprint 1949–1953	$14.95
2310	**Children's Glass Dishes, China & Furniture**, Vol. I, Lechler	$19.95
1627	**Children's Glass Dishes, China & Furniture**, Vol. II, Lechler	$19.95
4561	Collectible **Drinking Glasses**, Chase & Kelly	$17.95
3719	Coll. **Glassware from the 40's, 50's & 60's**, 3rd Ed., Florence	$19.95
2352	Collector's Encyclopedia of **Akro Agate Glassware**, Florence	$14.95
1810	Collector's Encyclopedia of **American Art Glass**, Shuman	$29.95
3312	Collector's Encyclopedia of **Children's Dishes**, Whitmyer	$19.95
3724	Collector's Encyclopedia of **Depression Glass**, 12th Ed., Florence	$19.95
1664	Collector's Encyclopedia of **Heisey Glass**, 1925–1938, Bredehoft	$24.95
3905	Collector's Encyclopedia of **Milk Glass**, Newbound	$24.95
1523	Colors In **Cambridge Glass**, National Cambridge Soceity	$19.95

4564	**Crackle Glass**, Weitman	$18.95
2275	**Czechoslovakian Glass** and Collectibles, Barta	$16.95
3882	**Elegant Glassware** of the Depression Era, 6th Ed., Florence	$19.95
1380	Encylopedia of **Pattern Glass**, McClain	$12.95
3981	Ever's Standard **Cut Glass** Value Guide	$12.95
3725	**Fostoria**, Pressed, Blown & Hand Molded Shapes, Kerr	$24.95
3883	**Fostoria Stemware**, The Crystal for America, Long & Seate	$24.95
3318	**Glass Animals** of the Depression Era, Garmon & Spencer	$19.95
3886	**Kitchen Glassware** of the Depression Years, 5th Ed., Florence	$19.95
2394	**Oil Lamps II**, Glass Kerosene Lamps, Thuro	$24.95
3889	Pocket Guide to **Depression Glass**, 9th Ed., Florence	$9.95
3739	Standard Encyclopedia of **Carnival Glass**, 4th Ed., Edwards	$24.95
3740	Standard **Carnival Glass** Price Guide, 9th Ed.	$9.95
3974	Standard Encylopedia of **Opalescent Glass**, Edwards	$19.95
1848	**Very Rare Glassware** of the Depression Years, Florence	$24.95
2140	**Very Rare Glassware** of the Depression Years, 2nd Series, Florence	$24.95
3326	**Very Rare Glassware** of the Depression Years, 3rd Series, Florence	$24.95
3909	**Very Rare Glassware** of the Depression Years, 4th Series, Florence	$24.95
2224	World of **Salt Shakers**, 2nd Ed., Lechner	$24.95

POTTERY

1312	**Blue & White Stoneware**, McNerney	$9.95
1958	So. Potteries **Blue Ridge Dinnerware**, 3rd Ed., Newbound	$14.95
1959	**Blue Willow**, 2nd Ed., Gaston	$14.95
3816	Collectible **Vernon Kilns**, Nelson	$24.95
3311	Collecting **Yellow Ware** – Id. & Value Guide, McAllister	$16.95
1373	Collector's Encyclopedia of **American Dinnerware**, Cunningham	$24.95
3815	Collector's Encyclopedia of **Blue Ridge Dinnerware**, Newbound	$19.95
2272	Collector's Encyclopedia of **California Pottery**, Chipman	$24.95
3811	Collector's Encyclopedia of **Colorado Pottery**, Carlton	$24.95
2133	Collector's Encyclopedia of **Cookie Jars**, Roerig	$24.95
3723	Collector's Encyclopedia of **Cookie Jars**, Volume II, Roerig	$24.95
3429	Collector's Encyclopedia of **Cowan Pottery**, Saloff	$24.95
2209	Collector's Encyclopedia of **Fiesta**, 7th Ed., Huxford	$19.95
3961	Collector's Encyclopedia of **Early Noritake**, Alden	$24.95
1439	Collector's Encyclopedia of **Flow Blue China**, Gaston	$19.95
3812	Collector's Encyclopedia of **Flow Blue China**, 2nd Ed., Gaston	$24.95
3813	Collector's Encyclopedia of **Hall China**, 2nd Ed., Whitmyer	$24.95
3431	Collector's Encyclopedia of **Homer Laughlin China**, Jasper	$24.95
1276	Collector's Encyclopedia of **Hull Pottery**, Roberts	$19.95
4573	Collector's Encyclopedia of **Knowles, Taylor & Knowles**, Gaston	$24.95
3962	Collector's Encyclopedia of **Lefton China**, DeLozier	$19.95
2210	Collector's Encyclopedia of **Limoges Porcelain**, 2nd Ed., Gaston	$24.95
2334	Collector's Encyclopedia of **Majolica Pottery**, Katz-Marks	$19.95
1358	Collector's Encyclopedia of **McCoy Pottery**, Huxford	$19.95
3963	Collector's Encyclopedia of **Metlox Potteries**, Gibbs Jr.	$24.95
3313	Collector's Encyclopedia of **Niloak**, Gifford	$19.95
3837	Collector's Encyclopedia of **Nippon Porcelain I**, Van Patten	$24.95
2089	Collector's Ency. of **Nippon Porcelain**, 2nd Series, Van Patten	$24.95
1665	Collector's Ency. of **Nippon Porcelain**, 3rd Series, Van Patten	$24.95
3836	**Nippon Porcelain** Price Guide, Van Patten	$9.95
1447	Collector's Encyclopedia of **Noritake**, Van Patten	$19.95
3432	Collector's Encyclopedia of **Noritake**, 2nd Series, Van Patten	$24.95
1037	Collector's Encyclopedia of **Occupied Japan**, Vol. I, Florence	$14.95
1038	Collector's Encyclopedia of **Occupied Japan**, Vol. II, Florence	$14.95
2088	Collector's Encyclopedia of **Occupied Japan**, Vol. III, Florence	$14.95
2019	Collector's Encyclopedia of **Occupied Japan**, Vol. IV, Florence	$14.95
2335	Collector's Encyclopedia of **Occupied Japan**, Vol. V, Florence	$14.95
3964	Collector's Encyclopedia of **Pickard China**, Reed	$24.95
1311	Collector's Encyclopedia of **R.S. Prussia**, 1st Series, Gaston	$24.95
1715	Collector's Encyclopedia of **R.S. Prussia**, 2nd Series, Gaston	$24.95
3726	Collector's Encyclopedia of **R.S. Prussia**, 3rd Series, Gaston	$24.95
3877	Collector's Encyclopedia of **R.S. Prussia**, 4th Series, Gaston	$24.95
1034	Collector's Encyclopedia of **Roseville Pottery**, Huxford	$19.95
1035	Collector's Encyclopedia of **Roseville Pottery**, 2nd Ed., Huxford	$19.95
3357	**Roseville** Price Guide No. 10	$9.95
2083	Collector's Encyclopedia of **Russel Wright** Designs, Kerr	$19.95
3965	Collector's Encyclopedia of **Sascha Brastoff**, Conti, Bethany & Seay	$24.95

3314	Collector's Encyclopedia of **Van Briggle** Art Pottery, Sasicki	$24.95
2111	Collector's Encyclopedia of **Weller Pottery**, Huxford	$29.95
3452	Coll. Guide to Country Stoneware & Pottery, Raycraft	$11.95
2077	Coll. Guide to **Country Stoneware & Pottery**, 2nd Series, Raycraft	$14.95
3433	Collector's Guide To **Harker Pottery** - U.S.A., Colbert	$17.95
3434	Coll. Guide to **Hull Pottery**, The Dinnerware Line, Gick-Burke	$16.95
3876	Collector's Guide to **Lu-Ray Pastels**, Meehan	$18.95
3814	Collector's Guide to **Made in Japan** Ceramics, White	$18.95
4565	Collector's Guide to **Rockingham**, The Enduring Ware, Brewer	$14.95
2339	Collector's Guide to **Shawnee Pottery**, Vanderbilt	$19.95
1425	**Cookie Jars**, Westfall	$9.95
3440	**Cookie Jars**, Book II, Westfall	$19.95
3435	Debolt's Dictionary of **American Pottery Marks**	$17.95
2379	Lehner's Ency. of **U.S. Marks** on Pottery, Porcelain & China	$24.95
3825	**Puritan Pottery**, Morris	$24.95
1670	**Red Wing Collectibles**, DePasquale	$9.95
1440	**Red Wing Stoneware**, DePasquale	$9.95
3738	**Shawnee Pottery**, Mangus	$24.95
3327	**Watt Pottery** – Identification & Value Guide, Morris	$19.95

OTHER COLLECTIBLES

2269	Antique **Brass & Copper** Collectibles, Gaston	$16.95
1880	Antique **Iron**, McNerney	$9.95
3872	Antique **Tins**, Dodge	$24.95
1714	**Black** Collectibles, Gibbs	$19.95
1128	**Bottle** Pricing Guide, 3rd Ed., Cleveland	$7.95
3959	**Cereal Box** Bonanza, The 1950's, Bruce	$19.95
3718	Collectible **Aluminum**, Grist	$16.95
3445	Collectible **Cats**, An Identification & Value Guide, Fyke	$18.95
4560	Collectible **Cats**, An Identification & Value Guide, Book II, Fyke	$19.95
4563	Collector's Encyclopedia of **Wall Pockets**, Newbound	$19.95
1634	Collector's Ency. of Figural & Novelty **Salt & Pepper Shakers**, Davern	$19.95
2020	Collector's Ency. of Figural & Novelty **Salt & Pepper Shakers**, Vol. II, Davern	$19.95
2018	Collector's Encyclopedia of **Granite Ware**, Greguire	$24.95
3430	Collector's Encyclopedia of **Granite Ware**, Book II, Greguire	$24.95
3879	Collector's Guide to **Antique Radios**, 3rd Ed., Bunis	$18.95
1916	Collector's Guide to **Art Deco**, Gaston	$14.95
3880	Collector's Guide to **Cigarette Lighters**, Flanagan	$17.95
1537	Collector's Guide to **Country Baskets**, Raycraft	$9.95
3966	Collector's Guide to **Inkwells**, Identification & Values, Badders	$18.95
3881	Collector's Guide to **Novelty Radios**, Bunis/Breed	$18.95
3729	Collector's Guide to **Snow Domes**, Guarnaccia	$18.95
3730	Collector's Guide to **Transistor Radios**, Bunis	$15.95
2276	**Decoys**, Kangas	$24.95
1629	**Doorstops**, Identification & Values, Bertoia	$9.95
4567	Figural **Napkin Rings**, Gottschalk & Whitson	$18.95
3968	**Fishing Lure** Collectibles, Murphy/Edmisten	$24.95
3817	**Flea Market Trader**, 10th Ed., Huxford	$12.95
3976	Foremost Guide to **Uncle Sam** Collectibles, Czulewicz	$24.95
3819	**General Store** Collectibles, Wilson	$24.95
2215	Goldstein's **Coca-Cola** Collectibles	$16.95
3884	Huxford's Collectible **Advertising**, 2nd Ed.	$24.95
2216	**Kitchen Antiques**, 1790–1940, McNerney	$14.95
3321	Ornamental & Figural **Nutcrackers**, Rittenhouse	$16.95
2026	**Railroad** Collectibles, 4th Ed., Baker	$14.95
1632	**Salt & Pepper Shakers**, Guarnaccia	$9.95
1888	**Salt & Pepper Shakers** II, Identification & Value Guide, Book II, Guarnaccia	$14.95
2220	**Salt & Pepper Shakers** III, Guarnaccia	$14.95
3443	**Salt & Pepper Shakers** IV, Guarnaccia	$18.95
4555	**Schroeder's Antiques** Price Guide, 14th Ed., Huxford	$14.95
2096	**Silverplated Flatware**, Revised 4th Edition, Hagan	$14.95
1922	Standard **Old Bottle** Price Guide, Sellari	$14.95
3892	**Toy & Miniature Sewing Machines**, Thomas	$18.95
3828	Value Guide to **Advertising Memorabilia**, Summers	$18.95
3977	Value Guide to **Gas Station** Memorabilia, Summers & Priddy	$24.95
4572	**Wall Pockets** of the Past, Perkins	$17.95
3444	**Wanted to Buy**, 5th Edition	$9.95

This is only a partial listing of the books on antiques that are available from Collector Books. All books are well illustrated and contain current values. Most of the following books are available from your local bookseller, antique dealer, or public library. If you are unable to locate certain titles in your area, you may order by mail from COLLECTOR BOOKS, P.O. Box 3009, Paducah, KY 42002-3009. Customers with Visa or MasterCard may phone in orders from 7:00–4:00 CST, Monday–Friday, Toll Free 1-800-626-5420. Add $2.00 for postage for the first book ordered and $0.30 for each additional book. Include item number, title, and price when ordering. Allow 14 to 21 days for delivery.

Schroeder's
ANTIQUES
Price Guide

. . . is the #1 best-selling antiques & collectibles value guide on the market today, and here's why . . .

Schroeder's ANTIQUES Price Guide

OUR #1 BEST SELLER!

Identification & Values Of Over 50,000 Antiques & Collectibles

8½ x 11, 608 Pages, $14.95

• *More than 300 advisors, well-known dealers, and top-notch collectors work together with our editors to bring you accurate information regarding pricing and identification.*

• *More than 45,000 items in almost 500 categories are listed along with hundreds of sharp original photos that illustrate not only the rare and unusual, but the common, popular collectibles as well.*

• *Each large close-up shot shows important details clearly. Every subject is represented with histories and background information, a feature not found in any of our competitors' publications.*

• *Our editors keep abreast of newly developing trends, often adding several new categories a year as the need arises.*

If it merits the interest of today's collector, you'll find it in *Schroeder's*. And you can feel confident that the information we publish is up to date and accurate. Our advisors thoroughly check each category to spot inconsistencies, listings that may not be entirely reflective of market dealings, and lines too vague to be of merit. Only the best of the lot remains for publication.

Without doubt, you'll find
SCHROEDER'S ANTIQUES PRICE GUIDE
the only one to buy for
reliable information and values.

COLLECTOR BOOKS
A Division of Schroeder Publishing Co., Inc.